Popular Mechanics

HOW TO TEMPT A FISH

WITHDRAWN

D0817084

Popular Mechanics

HOW TO
TEMPT A FISH

A COMPLETE GUIDE TO FISHING

The Editors of Popular Mechanics

HEARST BOOKS
A division of Sterling Publishing Co., Inc.

New York / London
www.sterlingpublishing.com

Copyright © 2008 by Hearst Communications, Inc.

All rights reserved. The written instructions, illustrations, and photographs
in this volume are intended for the personal use of the reader and may be
reproduced for that purpose only. Any other use, especially commercial use, is
forbidden under law without the written permission of the copyright holder.

Every effort has been made to ensure that all the information in this book is
accurate. However, due to differing conditions, tools, and individual skills, the
publisher cannot be responsible for any injuries, losses, and/or other damages
that may result from the use of the information in this book.

Book design by Barbara Balch

Library of Congress Cataloging-in-Publication Data
How to tempt a fish : a complete guide to fishing / The editors of
Popular mechanics [magazine].
      p. cm.
At head of title: Popular Mechanics
    Includes index.
    ISBN-13: 978-1-58816-726-2
    ISBN-10: 1-58816-726-7
1. Fishing. 2. Fishing--Equipment and supplies. I. Popular
>mechanics. II. Title: Popular Mechanics.
SH441.P8 2008
799.1--dc22

                         2007039686

10 9 8 7 6 5 4 3 2 1

Published by Hearst Books
A Division of Sterling Publishing Co., Inc.
387 Park Avenue South, New York, NY 10016

Popular Mechanics and Hearst Books are trademarks of Hearst
Communications, Inc.

www.popularmechanics.com

For information about custom editions, special sales, premium and
corporate purchases, please contact Sterling Special Sales Department at 800-
805-5489 or specialsales@sterlingpub.com.

Distributed in Canada by Sterling Publishing
c/o Canadian Manda Group, 165 Dufferin Street
Toronto, Ontario, Canada M6K 3H6

Distributed in Australia by Capricorn Link (Australia) Pty. Ltd.
P.O. Box 704, Windsor, NSW 2756 Australia

Printed in the United States

Sterling ISBN 13: 978-1-58816-726-2
          ISBN 10: 1-58816-726-7

CONTENTS

PREFACE

Remember how you felt when you hooked your first fish? Now, you can recapture that euphoria simply by paging through this book from the *Popular Mechanics* archives. Enjoy the advice from expert fishermen alongside the wonderfully enduring illustrations in this timeless guide to fishing first published in the 1950s.

Some of the tips are quaintly dated, such as how to make seating from an old garden hose, but many are still useful when fishing the streams of today. While manufacturers have made many technological advances, releasing better lures, rods, and reels, the sport of fishing itself has remained largely unaltered. At its core is our heart-pumping battle to land a big fish.

We've chosen to conclude this nostalgic collection with a serious article, originally published in 1984, that discusses the drastic changes in our lakes, streams, and shores since the 1950s. The importance of preserving our natural playground for ourselves and our children cannot be overstated.

We at *Popular Mechanics* hope you cherish this classic introduction to fishing in a simpler time.

The Editors
Popular Mechanics

INTRODUCTION

Some fisherman, who at least knew his geography, once claimed that "three-fourths of the earth's surface is water and one-fourth is land. It's clear the Good Lord intended a man should spend three times as much time fishing as he does plowing."

His logic does not seem so badly strained when we recognize the fact that well over 30 million Americans shared his view, at least partially, and went fishing last year. Already established as the world's most popular participation sport, fishing doesn't stop there. Statistics prove that its universal appeal is unsurpassed by any single spectator sport as well. Baseball fans: arise! But remember, many of you are also fishermen.

Let's just accept that when tens of millions of Americans enjoy anything, it must have appeal. But what makes fishing so popular? Communion with nature . . . peace, relaxation, quiet . . . good fellowship? Nonsense! A good pair of stout shoes and a bird-watcher's guide, a rest cure, and a bridge game would fill all of those requirements respectively. Happily, it so happens that all of these automatically become added fringe benefits of fishing—but hardly the real reason we do it.

How many of you have sat on a hard, wet seat in a cold drizzle for ten hours, bending a heavy oar through a choppy lake (to commune with nature)? How many have stood with half-frozen toes hooked around a slippery rock in the middle of an icy trout stream—braced for balance against a sweeping current—and made over a thousand casts in a normal day's fishing (for relaxation)? And how many of you have broiled yourself to the color and tenderness of rare beef—just to have the unleashed fury of a demented tarpon disdainfully zing your own lure past your already well-cooked ear (for peace)?

You know very well why you go fishing—and so do we. Of course, it's to catch fish, but—even more—isn't it always with the eternal hope that we tie into the BIGGEST member of whatever fish family we're after? Sure, we settle for what we get, and gladly so, but for most of us it's always "the biggest one that gets away." And that's what keeps us trying—wet seats, cold toes, insect bites, and all the other exquisite miseries we wouldn't trade for a uranium mine.

If the relatively minor rigors of fishing we mentioned above just to prove a point create some doubt in the mind of a would-be fisherman, we're sorry, but they are entirely true. In fact, we could add a great many more—and will. If you have decided by this time that fishermen must be more than slightly daft, you're probably right—because no one really understands fishermen, except fish and other fishermen.

Before you completely dismiss the idea of taking up fishing, please accept this sincere warning: don't, under any circumstances, let a supposedly good friend talk you into going with him to his favorite trout stream some sunny morning early in May. Because while you're sitting on the bank, watching spring seep into the countryside—when you can keep your eyes off the rippling, sun-sparked water—your friend may break his spell and yours. He might step out of the waist-deep stream with waders dripping and make the mistake of asking you to hold his 3½-ounce, extra-favorite fly rod while he stokes up his extra-smelly fishing pipe. Be careful—this is very dangerous. You gingerly hold the rod, paying no attention to the slack line drifting lazily down current toward a half-sunken log, then . . . WHAMMO! The rod take a deep bow toward the water, and only the instinct of reflex action makes you grab it with both hands. Luckily, one of them closes over the line, which was screaming off the reel. The rod tip again dips crazily, and now happens one of the most beautiful sights you'll ever see: a rainbow breaks the surface and walks on air . . . not once . . . not twice . . . but four times! And here is where your consciousness lets you feel the indescribable electricity that runs up that line into your arms—right down to your very toes! Now is also when you finally hear your supposed friend screaming at you, "Keep the tine light! Keep the tine light!" This garbled, well-meant advice at the top of his lungs seems as entirely natural as he is sitting waist-deep in water where you pushed him (but you don't remember when). You also don't remember how you wound up in the water yourself but you do know that you've hooked your first rainbow! As reason and calmness return, you start jabbering, "I gottem! I gottem! I gottem!" and go scrambling up the bank, dragging your prize behind you. Very normal, brother, very normal. Most of us did that—we understand completely. One catches his first fish only once.

Well, you got him. All yours—what a fighter, and what a beauty—all three-quarters of a pound of him! Don't worry, he'll grow. Before the end of the day he'll be "Oh, between a pound and a half and two pounds!" Only in this amazing fraternity, where members are born honest but soon get over it, can biology be so altered, permitting a fish to grow appreciably larger after its demise. Also, before the end of the day, while you are asking your supposedly good friend where he gets his tackle, you'll suddenly realize that your first fish wasn't the only one hooked this day.

C'mon in, brother—the water's fine!

Chapter 1

LURES

Are fishing lures designed to appeal to the fish . . . or to the fisherman? Walk up to any well-stocked tackle counter and you'll realize that this time-worn question is not always in jest. Running the gamut from awesome to zany, in an unlimited variety of shapes, sizes, and colors, the confusing array of available lures makes room for doubt quite understandable.

Before we can answer the question fairly, however, we must first try to understand fishermen. One accepted fact that will lead to this understanding is that a successful fisherman must think like a fish—at least to the extent of knowing the habits and preferences, as well as the habitat, of the species he seeks. Keep this in mind when you see some tanned, ruddy-faced individual haunting a lure display, drooling a little bit, with a somewhat glazed expression about the eyes. This will be a fisherman who, thinking like a fish, has developed their instincts to a high degree. In this sense, therefore, lures are designed for fishermen. On the other hand, if a lure doesn't appeal to a fish, it won't be on the market long—if it ever gets there.

Before we get into the problem of selecting lures out of this bewildering maze, it would be well to know a little more about them. Where do they come from, these weird bits of metal, plastic, glass, feathers, fur, and rubber in practically every imaginable shape and color? Do manufacturers keep a group of mad little men locked up in some dingy attic, turning out concoctions of a warped mind that resemble no living creature that ever walked, hopped, or crawled—let alone swam or flew? Perhaps someone sits in a bathtub carving up a bar of soap? No. In all seriousness, present-day lures offered by reputable makers are probably one of the most highly engineered items available to sportsmen today.

We're not talking about novelty or gimmick lures whose major value lies in the probability that they would frighten a fish to death or at least out of the water, where you could handily stone it on the bank. The reference here is to lures that are developed and designed with extreme care after a great deal of research and testing. That enticing wiggle, spasmodic twitching, or nervous flutter, which proves so irresistible to some game fish, doesn't just happen—a specific action or purpose is "engineered" into the lure! Just the right body circumference here, the exact degree of curvature there, the precise placement of the hooks, the specific gravity, plus hundreds of other details make the difference between a lure that simply "washes" through the water with no oscillation and one that really performs.

The same holds true for the selection of color patterns and finishes. These, too, are carefully determined after years of painstaking research and study. Limnologists, ichthyologists, biologists, entomologists, and scientists in many other fields all have contributed extensively to the factual knowledge that determines lure finishes and color patterns. Someone doesn't

ADVICE FROM AN ANGLER: Trout and other game fish can be caught on hooks baited with beads. For leaders, use fine copper wire and three hooks, each provided with a coral-colored band.

just run rampant with a few cans of paint in a vague hope that some startling combination will miraculously drive the fishing world mad. Add to this impressive list chemical engineers and their knowledge of curing, sealing, pigmentation, and plating—and you can appreciate that a good lure pattern today doesn't simply happen by accident.

COLOR PERCEPTION OF FISH

There is no longer any question about the ability of fish not only to see colors but to distinguish between them. Extensive experiments carried out by leading scientists such as Dr. Frank A. Brown of the Illinois Natural History Survey and other research groups—first with largemouth bass and then with other species—conclusively prove that these fish have good color perception. True, a fish's sight tends to be myopic, but exhaustive tests indicate that their vision is very similar to ours when looking through a compensating yellowish filter. In any event, experts agree that fish have remarkably clear vision at close range—more so than was common belief.

The color most readily visible to the fish tested progressed from the longer-wavelength portions of the spectrum, beginning with red, yellow, and orange, and decreased toward the blues and greens. Unquestionably, therefore, as the amount of light penetrating the water becomes filtered out, altering the ability to detect any color, not only the clearness of the water but the depth at which a lure is used will greatly affect its visibility.

At this point, you might well raise the question of colors and color patterns that do not even come close to resembling the natural food generally available to and sought after by fish. Good question. In this respect, we must take into consideration not only the feeding habits of fish but also their temperament. About half the time, fish strike because they are hungry or at least tempted to take a little tidbit, as do all of us. (This, incidentally, might partially explain the success of spinning, with its smaller lures.) In other cases, fish strike out of playfulness, curiosity, jealousy, anger, or fear. The last two emotions are probably incorporated into territorial defense. When we keep these motivations in mind, we can appreciate the importance of selecting a lure on the merits of visibility alone. Curiosity, for example, could readily account for the success of a light-reflecting spoon that may or may not simulate a silvery-sided minnow.

SOUND PERCEPTION OF FISH

What about conditions where visibility cannot be a prime factor in lure detection? Any number of conditions could contribute to this. It might be water depth alone, as mentioned previously, or turbid or cloudy water, an overcast day, or nightfall. Speaking of nightfall, and therefore of night fishing, we should keep in mind that a fish's eyes are made to gather light exceptionally well. And, as we know, in the open out-of-doors there is always some light, even on the darkest night. Because of this, many experts feel "that fish are every bit as color selective at night as on a bright, shiny day." We cannot find ourselves accepting this with any great degree of enthusiasm. Let's at least admit that color for visibility alone is no longer the prime consideration under these conditions.

Conclusive tests leave no doubt that fish have a highly developed sense of sound. With water being the excellent conductor of sound that it is, lures that create either an underwater sound or a surface disturbance noise come into their own when color visibility is reduced. Certain lures, therefore, are specifically designed for their sound-producing ability alone—such as poppers and plunkers, with their concave heads, or propeller-bladed surface plugs that buzz or thrash when retrieved. Incidentally, any lure that oscillates will produce an audible underwater sound, even if it is only the "clanking" of hardware.

We might conclude that when color perception is reduced for any reason, be it water depth, the lure's condition, or light, the body of the lure can still be seen in silhouette, and then shape, action, and sound predominate in the lure's effectiveness.

WHY SO SCIENTIFIC?

Right about here, someone is going to rear back with a disdainful snort and tell about his fishing buddy who fell off a pier, put his foot through the bottom of the boat, and, while neck-deep in water trying to rescue his sinking tackle box, caught the biggest bass of his life on the can opener.

We all know of cases where fish will hit on anything short of flopping up to your car and impaling themselves on the hood ornament. Sure, this happens every now and then—but let's be fair and honest: incidents like these are by far more the exception than the rule. Admittedly, some of the notable exceptions have had far-reaching effects. One outstanding case in point recalls that fine gentleman from Dowagiac, James Heddon, who discovered the effectiveness of an artificial plug by watching a bass strike savagely at a piece of wood he had whittled and tossed casually into the creek. The next day, he tried a similar piece of wood with a bottle cap forced onto the front and with hooks attached. It caught fish—and essentially the same plug still does.

Not exactly a scientific development, was it? No more than was Julio T. Buel's invention, some years prior to this, of the spoon lure—which incidentally is better named than we think, considering its origin. The story goes that Julio was enjoying his lunch while fishing one day and accidentally dropped a spoon into the water. He was sadly watching it wobble toward the bottom, when suddenly a large fish smacked at it. Although this led to the depletion of the family silver, it also resulted in the development of one of the most effective lures for catching fish today.

Another pioneer in lure development was Ivar Hennings, who, with a more scientific approach, spent many rain-soaked hours testing the effectiveness of a plug with a notched-out head. This caused it to submerge slightly and wobble enticingly when retrieved. Thus, the still-famous Bass-Oreno was born.

So what's all this fuss about scientific research and design? It's true that although the above lures and many like them were discovered more by accident than by design, they are still successful in attracting fish. This is because they were basically good for their purpose and still are. Why, then, the thousands of lures foisted on the fishing public today?

We must first accept the fact that any single given body of water—even completely disregarding changing temperature, weather, or light conditions—will produce enough different situations to require a basic variety of lures. Among these situations are depth, degree of clarity, amount of current—and, of course, where the fish are. Add that certain families or species of fish will respond more readily—because of mouth size, food preference, or habitat—only to certain families or types of lures.

Let's also admit that no one lure will produce a catch 100 percent of the time, even when used under identical circumstances. This may be partially explained by the fact that although fish are admittedly not smart, in the sense of actual brain power, they are wary. It is felt that many species will become "conditioned," at least for a time, to a lure that accounts for the disappearance or chagrin of too many fellow fish. There were not almost 40 million fishermen in America in those earlier days. Many an old-timer can tell you—and will—of taking fifty or more good-sized trout, in almost as many casts, from some still-famous hole that today may not produce three fish in a thousand casts. Your grandfather can tell you of the strings of lunker bass he would bring home every trip, while you settle happily for just not getting "skunked." Regardless of the reason—let's just say that because of more fishermen, there may be more conditioned fish—we do have to fish harder for what we get. And this is the reason reputable manufacturers continue to spend time, money, and effort on the research, development, and design of better, more effective lures.

In considering the relative importance of the lure as only one member of the tackle team that combines effectively to take sport fish, we cannot overlook the fact that it is the fish's first introduction to the fisherman. Those of us who have done even a moderate amount of fishing are well aware of how much importance fish attach to first impressions, and act accordingly.

Although we may have put the cart before the horse in discussing some background of lure design, we did want to establish a number of the reasons for the vast variety of shapes, sizes, and colors. Now let's get down to the lures themselves and try to clear up some of this confusion on how to go about selecting them.

HOW MANY LURES?

If anyone purchased only one of every available lure on the market today, he would need not only a trailer to get them down to the water, but a pretty full lifetime to try each one.

On the other hand, if one person were a combination meteorologist-astronomer-limnologist-ichthyologist and well versed in several other related sciences, he could conceivably purchase a single lure and produce a strike at his discretion. But before we congratulate this lucky fellow, keep in mind that he must take along with him one lure, a carload of instruments including a barometer, thermometer, and spectroscope, and a set of Solunar Tables, just to mention a few items.

Since very few of us would be inclined to fit into either of the above two categories, we will settle by making a selection of lures that will be adequate to suit an average number of fishing conditions—as well as our wallets.

One big step in solving the dilemma of a beginning fisherman making his first selection of lures is first to divide them into a few major classifications, based on the structural-functional features. This grouping will cover only the basic types in each category, since much of the confusion arises from comparatively minor modifications of the fundamental lure, be it by size, shape, color, or "fruit salad." If we understand the function of each family as well as how and for what species to use it, the basic selection problem should be largely solved. Then, if the novice should go out and buy a Goggle-eyed Squid-I-Diddee with the head and endowments of a mermaid, he has only himself to blame.

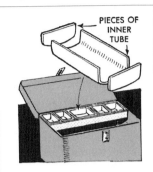

The enameled finish of casting plugs and the nickel surfaces of spoons and spinners will be preserved if a tackle box is lined with inner-tube rubber cut to fit and fastened in place with tire-patching cement. Silver-plated lures will tarnish.

THE SPOON-SPINNER FAMILY

This group not only represents one of the oldest of all artificial lures but is also probably the most universally used. It includes all lures in which the action results from water resistance against a dished-out surface or blade when it is being retrieved or trolled. The amount and type of action naturally depend on the depth of the dish, the general shape of the blade, and the speed it travels.

The two major divisions in this group are the wobbler spoon and the spinner. Generally, the spoon is thought of as being oval in shape—and most of them are. But any blade-type lure, usually with a bright, flashing surface, that wobbles, darts, and dives—but does not turn—falls into this class. Basically, wobbler spoons are classified by the manner of hook attachment, either fixed or free-swinging, and by shape.

A good example of the fixed-hook spoon is the Johnson Silver Minnow (Fig. 1). The Daredevil (Fig. 2) is a typical wobbler spoon with free-swinging hook. The Super-Duper and Trix-Oreno (Fig. 3, Fig. 4) are illustrations of spoons that deviate from the concept of symmetrical spoons but still fall into this class of wobblers. Although it can often be used to advantage with the addition of a pork rind or other "dressing," the spoon is considered

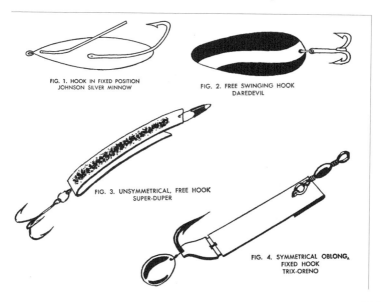

FIG. 1. HOOK IN FIXED POSITION
JOHNSON SILVER MINNOW

FIG. 2. FREE SWINGING HOOK
DAREDEVIL

FIG. 3. UNSYMMETRICAL, FREE HOOK
SUPER-DUPER

FIG. 4. SYMMETRICAL OBLONG,
FIXED HOOK
TRIX-ORENO

a "self-contained" lure. This is largely because it not only flashes intermittently but has an erratic action that simulates a wounded minnow or some other small fish. Most present-day spoons are made of metal, usually brass, and are plated in bright metal finishes for the flash attraction. Some are enameled in various color patterns, but the dished side usually remains bright. The most popular metal finishes are gold, silver or chrome, bronze or copper, and gunmetal. Although there are others, the red and white stripe seems to be the most widely used painted color pattern. There are probably hundreds of variations that incorporate feathers, bucktail or plastic skirts, as well as beads and propellers . . . but in keeping with our original promise to stick to basic lure types, the above gives us some understanding of the spoon family.

The spoon has a very high rating with most fishermen, and a selection of finishes should be in every tackle box, at least some with brighter surfaces, such as silver or chrome and white, for turbid (murky) waters or overcast days, as well as gold, bronze, and red for clear water and sunny days. Available in fly rod through saltwater trolling sizes, it has appeal for practically every species of freshwater and saltwater sport fish. The smaller sizes, with a fly or spinning rod, will take trout and panfish. Medium sizes (1/4 to 5/8 ounce) cast well for bass and walleyes as well as larger trout. The larger sizes (5/8 ounce and over), when trolled, have proved deadly for muskellunge, northern pickerel, and lake trout. Rate of retrieve when casting will vary among the spoon types and also depends on the action they

ADVICE FROM AN ANGLER: The next time you are trout fishing and none of your lures tempts the fish, smoke a spoon hook and cast it. The smoked spoon hook closely simulates a black bug or beetle, on which the trout feed.

produce. In general, however, too slow is better than too fast, and it doesn't hurt to let the lure "flutter" back to the bottom occasionally. So, for a lure that goes down deep when you want it to, the spoon, as an all-round fish getter, is hard to beat.

SPINNERS: These are first cousins to spoons in basic family resemblance but differ in that they consist of a blade or blades that completely rotate in a circular motion. There are four basic types of spinners, and they are classified mainly

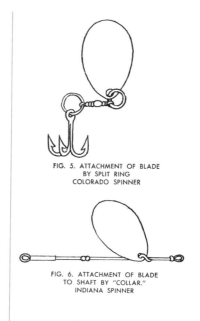

FIG. 5. ATTACHMENT OF BLADE
BY SPLIT RING
COLORADO SPINNER

FIG. 6. ATTACHMENT OF BLADE
TO SHAFT BY "COLLAR."
INDIANA SPINNER

by method of blade attachment and by number of blades, or "propeller" types.

In the identification of spinners by manner of blade attachment, there are three basic types. One is the blade that is fastened to a split ring to which the hook may be attached. The Colorado Spinner is an outstanding example of this type (Fig. 5). Obviously, since the blade rotates, it is necessary to attach a swivel above and below to prevent the twisting of your line and for free rotation.

The second type of blade attachment is best illustrated by the Indiana Spinner, wherein the blade turns around a shaft and is held by a clevis-type "collar" (Fig. 6). The third basic type is also attached to a shaft, but by a hole in the blade itself as well as with an arm that holds the blade out from the shaft at a fixed angle. The June Bug (Fig. 7) is most typical of this arrangement. One readily noticeable advantage of this "fixed-angle" type of spinner is that the blade starts to revolve with the slightest motion, whereas a certain speed is necessary to rotate the other types.

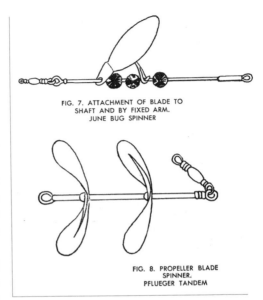

FIG. 7. ATTACHMENT OF BLADE TO SHAFT AND BY FIXED ARM. JUNE BUG SPINNER

FIG. 8. PROPELLER BLADE SPINNER. PFLUEGER TANDEM

The fourth and final classification of spinners is the twin-bladed or propeller type. In this group, one or two sets of blades are mounted on a shaft and rotate independently of it when moved through the water. The rate of travel, variation in blade shape, and pitch will affect the speed of rotation. Very often this type of spinner is incorporated with other lures—flies as well as plugs and spoons. In some cases, the propellers are used to rotate the entire body of a lure, as with the English Devon. For this category, however, we are concerned with just the basic propeller spinner (Fig. 8).

The primary purpose of the spinner group as a whole may be compared to that of a press agent or carnival barker. By their very nature, they do not cast as well as other, more compact lures but do an excellent job of announcing the enticement of "more to come." They are hardworking attention getters with their flash and oscillation, and when used ahead of other lures, bucktails, or even live bait, they do a very effective job. Used alone, the smaller-sized spinners work well for trout and pan-fish; the medium and larger sizes are ideal for deep trolling. Generally speaking, the selection of spinners, regarding finish and size, is governed by the same rules that control the choice of spoons.

THE PLUG FAMILY

The outstanding characteristic common to this group of lures is that they all have a "body," which in basic outline is reminiscent of a small fish. The current family name stems from the "plug" of wood out of which the original was carved. Although many plug bodies are still made of wood—red or white cedar being the most acceptable—the trend has been toward the use of plastics with low water-absorption qualities, such as Tenite.

In cases where intrinsic body shape or specific gravity is not relied on to control the lure's behavior, metal plates or blades and plastic scoops are incorporated to determine the plug's antics. As one of the most generally accepted groupings of plugs is based on the water depth at which they travel when retrieved, they are classified as surface, sub-surface, and sinking. They are also referred to as floaters, floater-divers, and deep running.

SURFACE PLUGS: As the name implies, these lures not only float but remain on the surface even when drawn through the water. Since they do remain on the surface and are better seen in silhouette, the actual color is not as distinguishable as is the strong contrast of a light and dark color combination. As their major function is to resemble something struggling on the surface, action and sound-producing qualities are the most important considerations. The classification of surface plugs is therefore based on the manner in which they obtain their action and how they produce a disturbance.

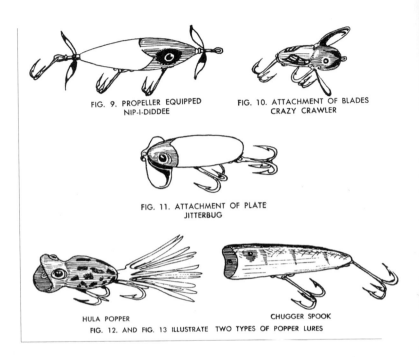

FIG. 9. PROPELLER EQUIPPED
NIP-I-DIDDEE

FIG. 10. ATTACHMENT OF BLADES
CRAZY CRAWLER

FIG. 11. ATTACHMENT OF PLATE
JITTERBUG

HULA POPPER

CHUGGER SPOOK

FIG. 12. AND FIG. 13 ILLUSTRATE TWO TYPES OF POPPER LURES

There are relatively few surface plugs that rely purely on action—usually imparted by the rod tip—without sound. When a planing surface is added to impart the action, it generally creates some gurgling or bubbling sound. The action-but-no-sound surface plugs are torpedo or cigar shaped and are used to best advantage in clear water and on bright days. The surface-disturbance or sound producers can be broken down into three main groups: plugs equipped with one or more sets of propeller blades, bodies with planing surfaces attached, and plugs with dished or concave heads—referred to as poppers or plunkers.

A prime example of the propeller-type surface plug is the Nip-I-Diddee (Fig. 9). Lures of this type have little or no wobbling action, but the propeller blades purr, buzz, or thrash—depending on the rate of retrieve. Two of the many lures that fall into the category of floaters that produce sound and action by the attachment of blades or plates are the Crazy Crawler and the Jitterbug (Fig. 10, Fig. 11). Because of their construction, these lures create a real hullabaloo when drawn along the surface: either a frantic paddling and splashing effect or a desperate gurgling and bubbling sound. The popper group, well named because of the popping or chugging sound they make, are best indicated by the Hula Popper and Chugger Spook (Fig. 12, Fig. 13). The popper type requires more rod-tip action for proper performance than do the other two groups of surface plugs, which can be "sent through their paces" by rate of retrieve alone.

Surface plugs are a must for bass, pike, pickerel, muskies, and, in appropriate sizes, trout, panfish, and innumerable saltwater species including weakfish, stripers, snook, and tarpon. They are most productive at night, with early morning next and then evening—in other words, at the time of day or season when fish may be inclined to feed on or near the surface. They should be cast as closely as possible into shoreline pockets, around stumps and sunken logs, into weed-bed openings—and, at night, along sandy shallows. Let the plug remain perfectly still after the cast, then twitch or move it only a few feet, keeping all the slack out of your line. Alternate this method with a fast retrieve, causing all the commotion that the lure is capable of making, and then cast it again in the same spot.

SUB-SURFACE PLUGS: This group shares the faculty of floating when at rest but digging under the surface, to varying degrees, when retrieved. When there is sufficient sunlight to penetrate below the surface, the color of these lures has equal importance to their action and shape. Considering that even in murky waters certain colors have higher visibility than others, the water's condition should determine your selection of color patterns.

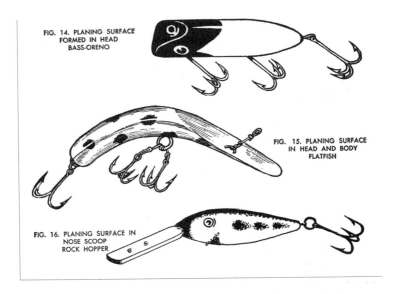

FIG. 14. PLANING SURFACE FORMED IN HEAD BASS-ORENO

FIG. 15. PLANING SURFACE IN HEAD AND BODY FLATFISH

FIG. 16. PLANING SURFACE IN NOSE SCOOP ROCK HOPPER

Here again, the structural features, which cause the lures to perform as they do, determine their classification within the group. There are three general divisions of sub-surface lures. The first consists of those with a planing surface formed into the head of the plug, much like the Bass-Oreno (Fig. 14). This type of design not only causes the lure to submerge just below the surface, but also imparts a swimming motion throughout the body. The Flatfish (Fig. 15) best illustrates the second division, in which practically the entire body of the lure provides the planing surface that controls its diving ability and action. The third basic division of sub-surface lures includes those that have diving plates or scoops either attached to or incorporated within the body itself. These plates are generally in the head or throat of the plug and in most cases cause a much greater depth penetration than the first two types mentioned. A typical example of a scoop-equipped floater-diver is the Rock Hopper (Fig. 16). This particular lure enjoys the versatility of a dual setting for either deep or shallow running.

To what fish will the sub-surface plugs best appeal? The same as those mentioned in connection with surface plugs: in other words, practically all game fish, depending on their feeding zone and temperament at the time the appropriate size is presented. Because the performance of this particular subdivision of plugs depends so completely on motion, the rate of retrieve and rod-tip action are highly important. Floaters will float when left alone and sinkers will sink without help, but sub-surface plugs will not submerge unless moved. A fast retrieve, with a lot of line out, will usually cause the plug to travel deeper—so vary the speed of the retrieve even on the same cast. Add some rod-tip action to give the lure a darting motion, and do not be afraid to pause occasionally. At all times, be sure all slack is out of the line so you have immediate control of the lure when you feel a strike.

SINKING PLUGS: Possessing no buoyancy, the plugs in this class will sink when at rest, at a speed that depends on their specific gravity. Because of the depths at which such plugs are often fished, their action, shape, and sound, in most cases, are more important than actual color for detection. However, marked color contrasts or "luminous" finishes have merit when used on sinking plugs.

As with the other two types of plugs, the manner in which these plugs attain their action or sound is the basis of classification within this group. There are also three general divisions of sinking-plug lures. The first are equipped with propeller blades that create both sound and flash but do not necessarily dart or wobble. The Torpedo (Fig. 17), appearing much like a surface brother, is a good example of this class. Second are those characterized by some planing surface, be it in the head of the body itself, by plates, or by a combination of the head and body that creates the lure's action, such as the Fish-Oreno (Fig. 18). The

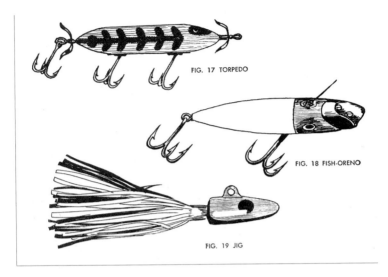

FIG. 17 TORPEDO

FIG. 18 FISH-ORENO

FIG. 19 JIG

third kind is exemplified by the Jig (Fig. 19). More head than actual body, these lures are roughly bullet-shaped metal with a skirt of feathers, bucktail, or plastic. With little or no built-in action of their own, Jigs depend mostly on the manner of retrieve or rod-tip action for effectiveness. Originating as a popular saltwater lure, they have successfully invaded certain types of freshwater fishing where a fast-sinking and deep-running lure is required.

Once more, the species of fish taken on sinking plugs is the same as those that fall victim to the surface plugs—with a special emphasis on walleyes. These plugs are particularly effective during the day or in warm weather when fish are inclined to be in deeper water. Here, too, the rate of retrieve should be varied and the lure allowed even to bump the bottom occasionally. In hot summer months, it is wise to try your lure at various depths if you find no action near the bottom. Very often, a lack of oxygen caused by the warming surface of the water will not permit fish to live beyond a certain depth.

SELECTION OF SPOONS
AND PLUGS IN GENERAL

You have probably concluded by now that the selection of spoons and plugs—be they surface, sub-surface, or sinking—is governed by the "feeding zone" of the particular species you are after at the time you are fishing. Here is where a knowledge of fish habits and fish lore in general must be your guide. Certain species will be "on the prod" because of the seasonal water temperatures they prefer—being active and feeding when it suits them, and completely uninterested when it does not. Each species will normally seek its own temperature-range preference and be found pretty much within it. Couple this fact with the current source of the species' natural foods, and you will at least have a starting point for where to expect to find them.

When arriving at any fishing site you are unfamiliar with, do not be afraid to ask local fishermen (as even the experts do), "What are they hittin' on?" They will be happy to tell you, and armed with their advice, you will be prepared to completely disregard it. Instead, get into the water and use your own common sense. You will probably do as well, if not better.

You will also learn more about your lures this way. Speaking of which, the manufacturer puts a lot of effort into preparing an insert that tells you exactly how that lure should be rigged and fished for best results. These instructions are prepared after extensive laboratory and field tests and are very factual. It just breaks the manufacturer's heart to have someone rip his new "world beater" out of the box, attach it to some weird mixture of snaps, sinkers, and swivels (which could ruin its action), and slosh it about in the water—understandably to be set aside soon as an "unproductive clunker."

SELECTION OF
LURES BY WEIGHT

Mention has been made of the variety of sizes of plugs and spoons to match the species of fish. This may be misleading and need some explanation. This reference was to the actual inability of a species, by the physical limitation of its mouth size, to take too large a lure; it was not made based on the outmoded belief that "big lures always take big fish." Spin fishing has probably done more than anything else to disprove this theory, because plenty of good-sized "lunkers" have been taken with the appreciably smaller spinning lures. Consider also the 30-pound rainbows to 80-pound salmon taken on small streaming flies or midget spoons and plugs.

When we speak of lure size, we more often mean its weight rather than the actual dimensions. As the type of fishing we plan to do—be it spinning, fly, or bait casting—predetermines the rod and reel we will use, the weight of the lure is matched to the ability of the rod and reel to handle it.

The line, too, has to be matched to balance this tackle team. In these three basic types of fishing, fly casting is the exception, in that the line is cast and the lure goes along for the ride. Here the line weight must be matched to the rod action. Although spinning and bait casting are allied, in that the weight of the lure takes the line from the reel, the basic difference in the principle of the reels brings any further similarity to an abrupt end. As this discussion is about lures, we will not go further into this point, except to conclude that the almost frictionless principle of the stationary line spool permits long casts with light lures, compared to the heavier lures needed to overcome the friction and inertia of the revolving bait-casting spool.

In a nutshell, then, with due consideration given to actual rod lengths and action, lure weights fall within the following ranges, unique to the many different styles of casting:

FLY-ROD SIZE: For those who use flyrods for spin fishing: the miniature editions of spoons, spinners, and plugs will vary from $1/20$ to $1/8$ ounce and usually require heavier-action rods than would a dry fly.

SPINNING SIZES: Starting with light-action rods and a line of 4- to 6-pound test, lure weights go from $1/8$ to $1/4$ ounce. Medium-action rods and 6- to 8-pound lines with lures ranging from $1/4$ to $3/8$ ounce are ideal for heavier freshwater fishing. Light-action saltwater spinning rods with 6- to 10-pound lines should handle lures from $3/8$ to $5/8$ ounce, and medium-action saltwater rods with 8- to 20-pound lines, $5/8$- to 1-ounce lures.

BAIT-CASTING SIZE: The average choice is $5/8$ ounce. Ultra-light bait-casting or spin-casting rods with a 6-pound test line will handle a $1/4$-ounce lure. Light bait-casting rods, with a line testing about 10 pounds, take lures from $3/8$ to $1/2$ ounce. Medium-action rods, with a 15-pound line, average $1/2$- to $3/4$-ounce weights, and heavy bait-casting rods, with a 20-pound line or over, will use $3/4$- to $13/4$-ounce lures for heavy freshwater fishing or saltwater casting.

As general as this review of the spoon-spinner and plug family has been, we hope that it may take some of the confusion out of the basic selection of lures. At least we have shown that certain lures do a specific job for a definite purpose.

Here are a few brief suggestions about taking care of your lures that will help keep them in the "win" column.

- Be sure your metal spoons and spinners are kept bright and shiny. As "flash" is their purpose, dulling and tarnish only defeat it.

- When rocks or strikes chip your painted plugs, touch them up with enamel or nail polish to keep them from further chipping.

• Never let hooks get rusty, and always keep them sharp. Occasional honing may make the difference between keeping or losing that "biggest one!"

THE FAMILY OF FLIES

The confirmed fly fisherman, with good reasons of his own, seems to consider himself a cut above all others and definitely the "aristocrat" of the fishing fraternity. Being somewhat short-necked, we will remain completely neutral on the subject—except to say that anyone who limits himself to only one phase of fishing is going to miss a lot of fun, as well as fish. Regardless of what stand any of us takes, it must be admitted that, of the three basic kinds of fishing, the proper handling of a fly rod is at least relatively more difficult to master. We also find within this group more hard-and-fast purists—to the point that a dry-fly fanatic won't even talk to a wet-fly user, let alone a "worm soaker."

In any event, fly fishing is considered by many to be the deadliest of all methods for taking fish. This may be due to the fact that most flies, and the way they are presented, probably come the closest to resembling the natural foods of the finny clan.

Any classification of the many hundreds of fly patterns within the main types of fly ties would take the courage and tenacity of a bulldog—and even then would probably be left unfinished in some padded cell. For our purposes here, only the basic kinds of flies available will be discussed—especially since preference for patterns varies so widely among both localities and individuals. The entire fly family can be divided into two basic groups: wet flies and dry flies. Wet flies are made to sink and dry flies to float. Although they may have an identical appearance and even the same name, wet flies are generally tied on somewhat heavier wire hooks, have softer hackles (the bristly "collar" around the head or body), and are not treated for repelling water absorption. The dry fly is usually tied on a lighter wire hook, has stiffer hackles, and is treated with a fly oil to help it float. It is conceivable that they can be interchanged if their floatability is switched.

There are, however, certain types of wet flies, such as nymphs, streamers, and bucktails, that by their nature would never be treated for surface use.

WET FLIES

NYMPHS: Wingless and very sparsely dressed with hackles, if any, these represent the last phase of an insect's development between the larval and adult stages. They are most effective when fish are feeding just off the bottom, to below the surface when the water first starts to warm in the early part of the season. Excellent for practically all trout, bass, and panfish, they should be fished slowly, near the bottom around rocks, and in eddies.

HACKLES: Also wingless, the hackles are a nymph form with more hackle tied around the head and somewhat more heavily wound bodies. Enjoying the distinction of being the oldest form of flies as well as the most widely popular, they are considered "all-seasonal" in appeal—color selection being matched to visibility and prevailing insect life at the time. Hair flies, which

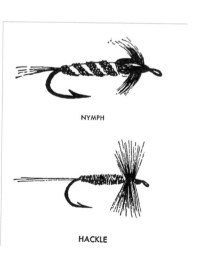

NYMPH

HACKLE

resemble hackles in construction, utilize hair rather than feathers and therefore remain somewhat stiffer and more bristly when wet. Another modification of the hackle fly is the Palmer Type, in which hackle feathers are wound throughout the length of the body, resulting in a fuzzy caterpillar effect. Such hackles get their name from an old English name related to a caterpillar, "palmerworm."

WINGED FLIES: This form of fly is divided into two basic types, closed wing and fan wing. The effect is obtained by the placement of the feathers. When the curved sides are turned outward, we have the "closed wing" effect; when reversed, the fan or "divided wing" is formed. This type of fly, when fished "wet," is supposed to represent a drowning insect, and it is put to best

advantage when warmer weather brings the fish closer to the surface. They come into use again when cooler weather sets in, egg laying is over, and dying insects are falling into the stream.

STREAMERS AND BUCK-TAILS: These are classed together because of general appearance and purpose; the principal difference is only that streamer flies are made of feathers and bucktails of hair. Normally longer and more streamlined, when wet they take on the appearance of a small minnow. Although

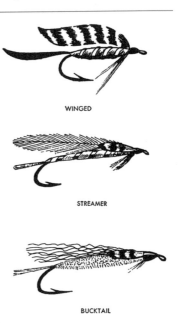

WINGED

STREAMER

BUCKTAIL

they can vary greatly in size, this type of fly is usually larger than average and has proved most successful for taking saltwater game fish as well as larger freshwater species. When used for large salmon or small tarpon, weakfish, bluefish, and mackerel, to mention a few popular saltwater varieties taken by this fly, it's always a good idea to have a comfortable amount of backing line on a large-capacity reel.

Because of their purpose, streamers and bucktails should be fished near the bottom and with plenty of action. It may sometimes be necessary to add weight to get them down in fast water. This type of fly also lends itself better to trolling than do others. In freshwater fishing, they are most effective in the very early part of the season, before nymphs start to emerge and fish are in deeper water, and again in late fall when they return to the bottom or lower levels of deep pools.

DRY FLIES

Many people have been prone to associate dry-fly fishing exclusively with the trout family. This is far from true. Many species of game fish, including walleyes and pikes, have risen to a fly, and it has taken too many bass and other sunfish to leave any room for doubt. It is true that some flies are constructed specifically to appeal to a certain species, such as bass bugs or panfish flies. Strictly speaking, some of these latter may be considered plugs because they have such a distinct "body." But as long as they also have wings and appendages of feathers or hair and are usually cast with a fly rod, let's classify them with flies.

In a sense, because dry flies are definitely surface lures, they are somewhat more limited in use than wet flies, considering that their effectiveness is only during those times of day or seasons when fish are feeding at the surface. Their great variety of forms

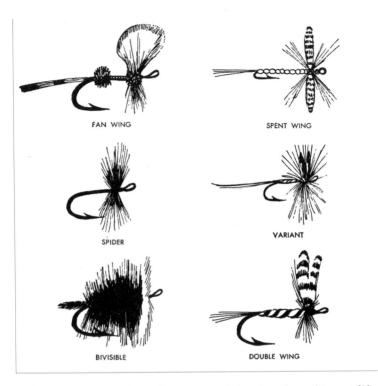

FAN WING

SPENT WING

SPIDER

VARIANT

BIVISIBLE

DOUBLE WING

and patterns stems from the same variety of preferred insect life. Although there are many dry-fly forms with many sub-modifications, for our purposes here we will list only the basic ones.

UPRIGHTS: Also known as parachutes, these are characterized by feathered wings, tied in an upright position, and by stiff hackles and stiff hair feathers that aid in floatability.

FAN WINGS: The curve of the wing feathers flares outward from the fly body and is larger and more rounded than wing feathers of the upright fly.

SPENT WING: Not as heavily dressed, this fly depends largely on wings that spread outward at right angles to the body for flotation. The wings are generally longer and narrower than most winged flies.

SPIDERS: These are wingless, and though tied much like the wet hackle fly, they have longer, thicker hackles and smaller hooks in comparison to their size.

VARIANTS: Tied much like the spiders, these have slightly shorter hackles and include two small wings—apparently to give a combination fly and spider appeal.

BIVISIBLES: In keeping with the name, these are tied with hackles of two contrasting colors. From the standpoint of color, they have a double value: the merit of visibility by contrast, and a choice of color.

DOUBLE WING: Almost exclusively for dry-fly use, these have two feathers tied closely to form each wing. With oil dressing added, they enjoy extreme buoyancy.

SELECTION OF FLIES

It certainly is not necessary, even if it were possible, to have every form and pattern of fly on the market. Used correctly in the right time and place, all of them will catch fish. Therefore, a moderate selection of patterns, based on regional preference, in several forms of wet and dry flies, should suffice for your average fishing needs. Remember, you can always decorate your hat with the things—so they will never be a total loss. In this respect, some fly patterns, especially salmon flies such as the Jock Scott, among many others, are downright dazzling in their beauty.

Many people make a hobby of collecting them for this reason alone. It is a good precaution never to put your flies away when wet; rot and rust will ruin the windings, and they will deteriorate very rapidly. It is also good to sprinkle some moth crystals over them when they are stored for any period of time.

CONCLUSION

It may have become apparent that there has been an almost studious avoidance of mentioning live bait in this discussion—to the point where it might be conspicuous by its absence. We certainly do not mean to deny the merits of this kind of fishing—under certain circumstances, its superiority. Live bait definitely has its place in sport fishing, and local preference would normally dictate its selection.

Perhaps at this point we should mention that although we should fish seriously, fishing—being the recreation and sport that it is—requires a good sense of humor to enjoy it completely. If we do not have one, the fish certainly do—as so well indicated by Edith Blanchard's little poem we saw somewhere entitled "Turnabout":

> *I fished all day without a bite*
> *No piscatorial glories*
> *But the fish sat up and laughed all night*
> *Telling people stories.*

So, to the original question, "Are fishing lures designed to appeal to the fish . . . or to the fisherman?" the answer is both, with a lot of fun in between. By the way, fellas, what are they hittin' on?

Chapter 2

TEMPT 'EM WITH LIVE BAIT

Bait fishermen are the boys who want above all else to bring some fish back. And it is generally true that, all other things being equal, you'll catch more fish with live bait than with artificial lures, even though some fishermen may think you sacrifice thrills and sport by so doing.

If live bait catches the most fish, at the same time it presents more problems—the bait must be caught and kept alive and frisky. In addition, you have to know your season, waters, and the kind of fish you are going after pretty well in order to establish whether the best bait will be worms, grasshoppers, crawfish, or some other form of live bait. A fly box will hold artificial lures covering many situations. But you can't take every kind of live bait along—you'll have to decide this before you start out.

ADVICE FROM AN ANGLER: The next time you have a hard time finding worms for fish bait, force the tines of a pitchfork into the ground and twang the handle. This creates vibrations that cause the worms to come up to the surface.

EARTHWORMS

Fishermen generally agree that there are only two kinds of worms fit for fishing—garden worms and night crawlers. Red worms, which are often called manure worms, are not fat enough to attract most fish, and their color is considered a drawback by some live-bait experts.

Garden worms are the kind you turn up with a pitchfork within a foot of the surface of your garden. They are ideal for still-fishing for small panfish. Not very hardy, they will have to be packed in cool, moist earth for the trip and carefully placed on the hook. They can't be bunched up on a hook as can the sturdy night crawlers.

Even in the most heavily-fished streams, trout find it difficult to resist a worm offered in either of these two ways. One successful method utilizes a twig with a leaf or two attached. After the worm-baited hook is pushed through the edge of the leaf, as in the upper detail, the twig is allowed to float downstream. When the leaf drifts over a likely pool, the hook is jerked free by a twitch of the rod tip. The bait then sinks slowly to the bottom, coaxing the trout into striking. The other method is to mold a ball of clay or mud over the worm and hook, as in the lower detail. The ball is lowered slowly into the water and washes away to expose the worm.

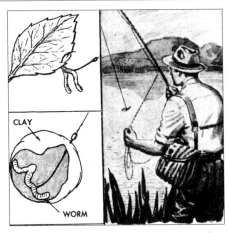

CLAY

WORM

Night crawlers can't be turned up with a pitchfork, since they burrow deep. But they emerge in numbers at night or in the daytime after a heavy rain. You can bring them out during dry weather by soaking the ground with a garden hose or sprinkling it with a solution of mustard and water.

Although worms are found in abundance on a freshly sprinkled lawn, they are hard to catch because they withdraw to their holes when a white light is flashed on them. If a square of red cellophane is fastened over the lens of a flashlight, the worms will be easier to approach, since they are not so sensitive to red light. The same is true of grasshoppers.

You can easily build your own "wormatorium" by utilizing an old washtub. Punch a row of holes around the lower part of its side and a number of holes in the bottom to allow for drainage. Cover the bottom of the tub on the inside with a piece of screen wire to prevent small worms from falling through the drain holes. Place a layer of corncobs, broken into short lengths, over the screen wire, next to a layer of well-rotted leaf mold and then a layer of rich soil. Repeat this procedure

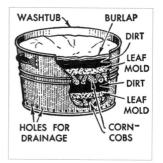

until the tub is nearly full, then lay several burlap sacks across the top. After dampening the contents of the tub, dig up a few hundred worms and place them under the sacks. Feed the worms every ten days with a mixture of 1 cup of coffee grounds, 1 cup of thick, sour milk, and 3 tablespoonfuls of syrup. The tub should be kept in a cool part of the basement during the summer months, and in a warm place; preferably near the furnace during the winter. Keep the contents of the tub damp but not too moist.

When using worms for fish bait, anglers will find that trout and bass are more apt to strike if the worms are kept fresh and

The problem of carrying a jar of salmon egg fish bait so it is easy to get at is solved with this simple holder, which slips over your trouser belt. Take an ordinary clothespin and screw a couple of strips of heavy sheet metal or spring steel onto it as indicated, making the top one so that it pivots easily. Then cut a notch in the pin just above the circular metal strip to take the edge of the jar lid. When you want to remove some of the eggs, just swing the pivoted metal piece to one side and take off the lid.

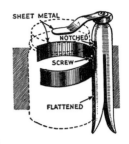

SHEET METAL
NOTCHED
SCREW
FLATTENED

firm. This is best done by lining the bottom of your bait box with swamp moss, which can be found in marshy woodlands—or obtained at your nearest florist. After covering the bottom of the bait box with moss, dampen it, place the day's supply of worms inside, and cover them with more moss. The worms will be firm and fresh when the stream or lake is reached, and they will remain in good condition for a full day's fishing.

MINNOWS

Next to earthworms, minnows are the most commonly used live bait. They are a more natural fish food, since all fish eat minnows as a part of their natural diet, while worms are not a common food of most fish. Minnows are relatively easy to find: they are present in almost all lakes, ponds, rivers, and streams. They are easily caught with traps, nets, or seines. Whichever method you choose will be even easier if you scatter cracker crumbs, bread crumbs, oatmeal, or some other appealing bait on the surface of the water. In the presence of food, minnows lose all caution.

You can make a minnow net that can be folded by splitting a length of bamboo pole and attaching a wire to one section to be used as a spread. The wire is looped at one end, to engage a hole in one leg of the pole, and given a double, right-angle bend at the other, to permit insertion into a hole in the opposite leg. The net is attached by sewing or by using waterproofed glue. When not in use, the pole is folded and the net wrapped around it.

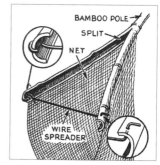

Transporting minnows is not difficult if they are kept in water that is not allowed to become warm. One way to keep the water cool in a minnow can or bucket is to invert a burlap sack over the can and push it down into the water. Pieces of twine hold the sacks in place, and small rocks are dropped into the pocket thus formed. The rocks keep the burlap immersed so that it can act as a wick to carry water to the portion exposed to the air. In that way, evaporation serves to keep the cans cool, and the splashing water helps maintain the necessary oxygen for the minnows.

Some fishermen prefer to preserve their minnows. This can be done with a solution of 1 part formalin to 100 parts of water. A tap on the head will kill the minnows, after which immerse them in the solution tail up and leave them for a week to ten days. Then drain off the solution and replace it with a fresh mixture, this time adding a little glycerin to keep the minnows from

ADVICE FROM AN ANGLER: If a minnow net or seine is to be waterproofed, it should be thoroughly dry before it is treated. The net is soaked for half an hour in raw linseed oil and spread over bushes or hung on a line to dry. Nets given this treatment will not absorb water, and after use they can be shaken to throw off moisture and then immediately packed away.

ADVICE FROM AN ANGLER: Minnows used as bait are often washed off the hook when fishing in swift water. By wrapping and taping a piece of cellophane around the line and sliding it down so that it covers the minnow on the hook, the bait will be preserved without affecting its efficiency as a lure. This may also be used to protect worms and grasshoppers.

stiffening. The minnows will keep in this indefinitely. A few drops of dye or food coloring are often added to give the minnows a pale yellow or red tint.

In fishing with live minnows, bait the hook so that the minnow will be as frisky as possible. Veteran fishermen prefer either hooking the little fish below the dorsal fin—be sure not to go deep enough to hit the backbone—or passing the hook through both lips.

CRAWFISH

This little cousin of the lobster is more properly called crayfish. Crawfish can be used whole as bait while in their soft-shelled stage. The hook is passed into the body from the underside of the tail. If this is done carefully, the bait will live and be lively for a considerable time.

In the hard-shelled stage, the crawfish tail, cut into suitable pieces, makes excellent bait for game fish.

Keep crawfish alive in this improvised "icebox." Pack the bottom of a pail with ice, then cover it with screen wire and a layer of grass. The crawfish are placed on top of the grass and, in turn, covered with several thicknesses of newspaper and wet burlap sack.

Although a few crawfish may be seen during the daytime, the best time for catching them is at night, when they come out of their homes among rocks and underwater brush to feed. Seining is the most commonly used method of catching them, although crawfish will enter a wire minnow trap baited with dead fish or meat.

The difficulty of seining crawfish from a pond or stream that contains vegetation, where they usually are plentiful, is eliminated with this seine, which consists of a wooden scoop having a burlap sack at the rear end. If the seine has a tendency to float or not rest heavily enough on the bottom of the pond to flatten the growth as it is pulled along, weight it with a stone or heavy piece of metal. Drilling a number of small holes in the bottom of the scoop also will help it sink to the bottom.

GRASSHOPPERS

Grasshoppers are natural fish food, since many of them often misjudge their leaps and fall into streams and lakes. It follows that they make excellent bait for casting lines. They are particularly good as bait for fish that take food from the surface of the water. The grasshopper is bound to the inside curve of the fishhook shank with a silk thread. Place it belly down in

A tobacco can makes a handy container for carrying live grasshoppers. An oblong hole is cut in the top, which is closed by means of a slide cover. The guides in which the slide works are soldered to the top of the can, which can be carried in a jacket pocket.

the curve of the hook, then pass the thread around the carapace, or tough collar, of the insect.

Don't try to catch grasshoppers in the daytime—that's for the birds. But at night the grasshoppers become torpid and chilled and can be found easily with a flashlight and picked off the rocks and grass to which they cling. Keep them in a wire-mesh cage—you can easily fashion one yourself—and add a few handfuls of grass to keep them fresh and lively.

FROGS

There's no better bait for largemouth bass and the large varieties of pike than frogs. Catch them at night, using a strong light with a good reflector. The light will blind them, and they will be easy to pick up onshore or in shallow water. In narrow, deep waters, a seine or long-handled frog net will be best.

A five-gallon oilcan provides an excellent "net" for catching frogs. The top and bottom of the can are cut away, and a wooden handle is nailed between two sides at the top. When a frog has been sighted, the can is quickly put over it.

When the frog is to be used as live bait, it should be hooked through both lips, leaving the legs free to swim. Many fishermen hook them through the skin of one leg, but their swimming movements are then hampered and unnatural. This is sometimes best, however, for small fish that would attack only an injured frog.

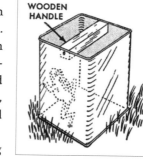

Frogs can be kept lively for a long time if they are cool and moist. Carry them in a minnow bucket, half filled with fresh grass and with about an inch of water covering the bottom. For short trips, frogs can be put in a mesh bag, or even an old stocking.

HELLGRAMMITES

This black, hairy little insect, with six legs and four wings, makes an excellent bait for bass, and it sometimes causes trout to rise. Hellgrammites can be found on the underside of stones, logs, and other rubble in swift-running streams. They are easily gathered but very hard to keep, since they are not very hardy; they will rarely stay alive overnight. The hellgrammite has a tough, wide collar at its neck. Run a fine hook underneath this collar, taking care not to go so deeply as to kill the bait.

ADVICE FROM AN ANGLER: When natural fish bait, such as minnows, grasshoppers, and other insects, is plentiful, it can be dried and preserved for future use. To do this, just bait a number of hooks, immerse them in collodion, and then lift them out and dry them. This coating is tough and waterproof and excludes air.

CRICKETS

Here's an excellent bait, but one that's extremely hard to catch no matter what time it is. Unlike the grasshopper, the cricket does its traveling at night. During the day, it rests under stones and logs, but it is extremely agile about eluding capture. Some very fast work with a light net is necessary to catch a respectable number of crickets. They do not live well either in a bait bucket or on the hook, but they are effective bait even when dead. The hook is run through the middle of their bodies, and often two or three are placed on a single hook.

> Keep live grasshoppers or crickets in a jar with a piece of inner tube stretched tightly over its top. Cut a slit in the inner tube wide enough to permit you to insert your thumb and forefinger for grasping.

PORK RIND

This bait is neither alive nor a natural food of fish, yet it has been found to be tremendously effective and is usually classed among "live baits." Strips of pork, which may be bought already preserved in jars or tins, have an enticing wiggle when in the water. Because pork is edible, the fish do not tend to eject it from their mouths after striking. And because of the tough rind, pork bait is the least likely of edible baits to be pulled from the hook. It is sold in strips or wedge-shaped chunks. Either of these forms moves in a lifelike manner when reeled in from a cast.

Chapter 3

CARE AND REPAIR OF YOUR ROD

No matter how much you spend for your fly or bait rod, it's not going to do a proper job for very long unless you take care of it. In fact, the better and finer your rod, the more attention it is going to require keeping it in tip-top shape.

GUIDES

Handle and store your rod carefully to avoid injury to the guides. If a guide becomes bent or flattened, it can be repaired easily with a pair of needle-nose pliers, handled gingerly. If the guide becomes unseated, however, repairs are more troublesome. On a bamboo rod, the old wrappings must be cut off and

ADVICE FROM AN ANGLER: The next time you have to replace the winding on your fishing rod, try fine copper wire instead of silk thread. The wire will last longer and produces a neat appearance when carefully wrapped. A drop of solder melted over the windings and smoothed with a hot iron seals the ends.

Bamboo fishing rods may be identified permanently with your name or initials. First, rub a small area of the rod with fine steel wool to remove the varnish, then write on this part with India ink. After the ink has dried, cover it with varnish.

the guide rewound to the rod. On graphite rods, unseated guides can sometimes be reseated with solder. A broken guide is a case for the manufacturer's repair department.

SEASONAL CARE

Bamboo rods should be gone over at the end of every season. All frayed wrappings should be replaced, and in some instances the entire rod will need to be rewound. The varnish should be rubbed down with oil and pumice, and one or two coats of new varnish may need to be applied, rubbing down between coats if the second is applied. Apply the varnish with a bristle brush in a warm room. Dry the rod in the most dust-free spot you can find. Keeping the rod well varnished is the best means of avoiding dry rot and warping. A well-cared-for bamboo rod does not need to be revarnished every season, especially if it

ADVICE FROM AN ANGLER: If the inside surfaces of the ferrules of your casting rod are polished with a piece of wax paper, the rod is not likely to stick at the joints when you take it apart.

has been put away dry and stored correctly in its case.

FERRULES

The male and female ferrules by which the jointed rod is brought together are the principal fittings of the fly or bait rod.

They are found primarily on bamboo rods these days. Most modern rods have graphite sleeves or spigot ferrules that are built as part of the rod blank, which allows for a very smooth transfer of action from one section of the rod to another.

Ferrules should be checked carefully for workmanship when buying any kind of rod. They are capped, or shouldered, on the outside of the

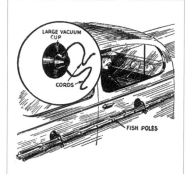

Long fishing poles can be carried on the side of a car without marring the finish by tying them to a couple of large vacuum cups attached as shown. It is not necessary to remove the cups while on a fishing trip, as they do not interfere in any way with opening and closing the doors. For exceptionally long poles, attach an extra vacuum cup on the front fender so that the pole ends can be tied.

rod to ensure a perfect joint. On some older types of rods, the ferrule is also held by a small steel pin, but these are regarded as a nuisance by many fishermen and are discarded the first time ferrule repairs are made. The best ferrules are serrated, to give a good grip between rod joints. They should be given a waterproof finish by the manufacturer, and most of them are.

At the end of a fishing season, ferrules on some bamboo rods are apt to become loose. This is indicated by a slight knock heard when casting or wiggling the rod. This means that either

ADVICE FROM AN ANGLER: Cutting-rod ferrules can be tightened in a jiffy as follows: take the rod apart, lay the section with the outer ferrule on a solid object, and strike the shell sharply at several points with the back of a table knife. This will make little dents, scarcely noticeable, which will cause the ferrules to fit snugly.

the cement holding the ferrule inside the rod has loosened or the wood has dried and shrunk. In either case, the ferrule must be removed and reseated. Because of the high cost of quality bamboo rods, it's often prudent to have it repaired professionally.

STORAGE

The fisherman who carelessly stacks his equipment in a closet or the corner of his garage is doing more damage to the delicately constructed tackle than could be done by years of fishing. Some means of storage should be afforded that will give protection to rod tips, guides, and ferrules. There are several tried-and-true methods of storage besides the obvious one of buying an expensive rod cabinet. A storage cabinet can be made from a length of eaves trough. End pieces are soldered to the trough, the upper one being slotted to allow the rod tips to stick

FISHING ROD

SHADE-ROLLER BRACKET

A handy bracket for hanging a fishing rod on a wall can be had by utilizing a window shade bracket as shown. The bracket is nailed to the wall, and the slot is enlarged so that the tip of the rod is easily slipped in. The edges of the slot should be smoothed with fine abrasive paper to avoid marring the finish on the rod tip.

Here's a simple way to carry your long fishing poles on top of a car safely without scratching the paint. Just obtain a couple of plungers, cut off part of the handles, and fit metal clips on them as shown. These can be cut and bent from a discarded clock spring or a piece of spring steel.

Merely press the cups onto the car top, slip the poles in place, and then tie the pole ends to the radiator ornament and rear bumper, which prevents them from whipping or sliding the clips.

through. A couple of hinges and a padlock hasp are soldered on for attaching the cabinet to a wall and locking it. Finish with good metal paint.

A good hanger for a fishing rod can be made by simply tacking a short length of rubber hose to a wall at an angle. The rod is inserted into the hose, and its tendency to hang vertically will cause the tip to bind at the top and keep it from slipping out

ADVICE FROM AN ANGLER: To protect a valuable fly when carrying a casting rod through weeds and brush, you can cut a slit in the side of a hollow rubber ball and slip it over the fly, letting it dangle from the tip of the rod. Another method is to impale the ball on the rod near the grip so that it will always be at hand for the same purpose.

of the hose. Such a hanger has the advantage of not injuring the agate tip, no matter how carelessly the rod is inserted.

Another good hanger that will hold several rods can be fashioned from a bookkeeper's spring-type penholder. Screw the holder to the wall and hang the rods between the springs by their tips.

Fishing rods of the one-piece type can be protected against rough handling by inserting them into a length of thin-wall steel tubing. The tubing is cut to the required length, and both ends are closed with rubber crutch tips.

The agate tips of old fishing rods can be protected by cutting a piece of bamboo to slip over the tip, or inserting a tiny cork inside the tip guide. The latter method also provides a method of shielding a hook by sticking the point into the projecting end of the cork.

An ordinary cardboard tube of the proper length and diameter is readily converted into a handy case for carrying two or three fishing rods. Impregnate the rod with hot paraffin, applied with a brush. Then take two tin cans of the proper diameter, remove the tops, and slip them snugly over the ends to provide a cover and bottom for the case. The bottom can should be cemented so that it will not slip off, and the top should afford a snug but sliding fit. Then wrap the tube between the cans with a tight winding of fishing line. Also wrap the outside of each can. Give the entire assembly several coats of varnish or shellac.

ADVICE FROM AN ANGLER: Desiring to carry a long fishing pole on a trailer, one motorist put a length of conduit on the underside of the trailer and inserted the pole into it. The conduit was attached with pipe straps, and the ends were capped to keep the pole in place.

Chapter 4

REEL NEEDS
CARE AND SERVICE

To the fly fisherman, a reel is the least important part of his equipment. Since he feeds out the line with his left hand in casting, the reel serves only as a convenient holder for the line, as well as a means of retrieving it after the cast.

It is in bait casting that the reel comes into its own. Here the reel is a precision instrument, and balance, jeweling, multiplying ratios, and such features as anti-backlash and level-winding mechanisms become important.

The best reels are made of stainless steel or plated nickel, with bronze bearings and bushings. The more expensive ones have bits of agate, garnet, or sapphire

ADVICE FROM AN ANGLER: Slipped over the handles of your fishing reel, a couple of ordinary penny pencil erasers will enlarge the handles so that you can grip them with less finger strain when reeling in the line. The shape of the grip may be altered to suit your individual taste by cutting off some of the rubber with a sharp knife. No cement is needed, as there is plenty of grip.

set in the center of the oil cap to reduce friction, and other jewels are set in holes in the bushings. Today's reels are often strikingly beautiful, with their frames and head-cap rings inset with plastics of brilliant colors and markings.

CLICK AND DRAG

Most bait-casting reels are quadruple multiplying—that is, the spool revolves four times to one turn of the handle. Practically all are equipped with a click—a pawl and ratchet controlled by a thumb button. The click keeps the line from running out while the rod is being carried or otherwise handled while not casting. The line can be cast with the click on, and some beginners leave it on for short casts. But this practice will soon wear out the click; besides, it is bad training for longer casts without the click. A stronger braking mechanism is the drag, also operated by a thumb button, which has no value from a casting standpoint.

ANTI-BACKLASH

More important from the casting standpoint are anti-backlash mechanisms. Fishermen used to have to stop the movement of the reel by pressing their thumb on the line just as the bait hit the water. If this was not done at that precise moment, the momentum of the free-running reel resulted in a badly fouled line. This often happened just as the fisherman had a strike, and it resulted in many a lost fish. Anti-backlash mechanisms have largely eliminated tangled lines as a result of a cast. There are two types of anti-backlash mechanisms favored by fishermen. One has a wire bail, or brake, which is held up and off as the line goes out. As the bait drops toward the water and the line loses momentum, the bail drops gradually and applies partial pressure on the line. As the bait hits and the line stops, the brake falls over the unreeled line, and the brake is on completely. The tension of this mechanism can be regulated by a thumbscrew, and thus it can be adjusted to baits of varying weight. The other anti-backlash mechanism operates by means of small disks in the end plate of the reel. These expand by centrifugal force when the spool is in motion, and they contract to act as a brake when the spool slows down.

LEVEL-WINDER

The level-winder is a mechanism that automatically moves back and forth across the reel as the handle is turned, laying the line on the spool evenly. The convenience of this feature is well worth the investment for any fisherman.

FREE-SPOOL REELS

Many expert anglers favor a free-spool reel—one whose handle remains motionless when the cast is made and while the line is running out. Friction is reduced to a minimum

If you're more interested in how old a fish is than how big it is, count the rings on the scales. As in the case of trees, these rings indicate annual growth, there being one ring for each year. It may be necessary to use a magnifying glass to see the rings clearly. It should be remembered, however, that this is not an exact index and does not apply to all species of fish.

in free-spool reels. But there is one serious disadvantage: the gears must be engaged for retrieving the line either by pressing a thumb button or by pushing in on the end plate of the reel. If you forget to do this in the excitement of hooking a fish, you will find yourself feverishly winding a handle that turns nothing while the fish runs away with your line.

CLEANING

Dirt and sand are the archenemies of the reel. For this reason, it is important that any reel you buy be of three-piece take-down construction to allow you to clean and oil the parts regularly. In this type of construction, the spool caps and pillars are removable and the reel comes apart in three pieces—the head plate with crank and gear and drag, the tail plate with click spring and pawl, and the spool with pinion and click ratchet.

Before taking your fishing reel apart to clean and oil it, scribe a couple of circles on a piece of wood to simulate the ends of the reel, and drill holes to represent the screw positions. Then place the screws and small parts in the holes, so that you will not lose them or mix them up.

Set the drag before taking the reel apart. A jeweler's screwdriver, which has a ratcheted handle, is handy here. Wash the parts in benzene, gasoline, or naphtha. A soft rag or a piece of chamois should be used to clean out the pivot and gear holes. An old toothbrush can be put into service to scout away accumulated grit and grease. Put one drop of oil in the pivot holes and one in each gear

Extra hooks can be kept handy by sticking them in a cork and clipping them to your hatband. The clip is a bobby pin with one prong bent and inserted through the cork, leaving the other one to serve as a clip over the band.

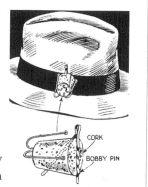

mounting. More oil than this can slow down a reel and cause trouble. Then grease the gears lightly with petroleum jelly or mutton tallow.

The reel should be reassembled carefully. Screws should be tightened a little at a time, giving each screw a slight turn alternately. Test the spool for end play, and stop tightening when the play is eliminated.

SLIP RINGS

Sometimes trouble develops with the slip ring, into which the tongue of the reel slips for mounting on the fishing rod. If the slip ring becomes loose enough to slide away from the reel, you can secure it by applying a drop of solder to the tongue of the reel over which the ring slips.

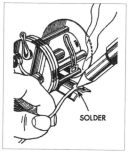

This will increase the size of the tongue and make the ring fit tightly. If the drop of solder is made slightly oversize, it can be filed down to ensure a good fit.

Sometimes the slip ring works loose from the rod, causing the reel to become wobbly or even to drop off while playing a

One of the simplest vises for tying fishing flies may be made from a pair of pocket tweezers with pieces of rubber tubing slipped over the tips. By pushing the handle of the tweezers through a narrow slit in the top of the tackle box, the points may be made to close and hold the hook firmly in any desired position.

fish. This can be avoided by fitting the ring with a thumbscrew. Drill a hole through the ring and solder a nut over it. Then turn the screw into the nut and against the rod tightly enough to afford a firm mounting.

REEL ARBORS

Most bait-casting reels have a capacity of from eighty to one hundred yards of line. Except when trolling, few fishermen ever use this much line. If only the amount of line customarily used is reeled up, however, the reel spool will tend to backlash because of insufficient weight. This can be avoided by first reeling on fifty yards or so of cheap heavy line, then following with good line. A drawback to this practice is the nuisance of drying the cheap line along with the good line. For a little extra, you can buy a cork arbor for your reel diameter and add enough weight.

Fishermen who occasionally troll from a boat, with a consequent need for longer line, can build up an arbor of old line that can be used when needed. Reel on the new line, then follow it with old line until the spool is filled to the capacity desired. Then unreel and reverse the lines, reeling up the old line first, tightly and evenly. Cut it off near the reel plate and wrap wide adhesive tape tightly around it. Three overlapping strips will usually do the trick. Give the tape two or three coats of shellac to make the arbor waterproof. Then reel on the new casting line. When you want to troll or otherwise use more line than usual, simply cut away the adhesive tape with a sharp knife and tie it to the new line ahead.

DRY-CELL TERMINAL CLIP, SOLDERED

Soldered to the edge of your tackle box, a clip from a dry cell provides a handy vise for holding a hook while tying a fly. Such a vise is always available even when you are on a fishing trip.

PROTECTION

A fine reel should be protected at all times. It should have a padded receptacle of its own in your tackle box, and it

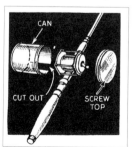

CAN

CUT OUT

SCREW TOP

should be given some sort of shield when being carried in the open. A handy metal shield can be contrived from a screw-top can, which is ideal for the purpose. The can is slotted along one side to slip over the reel, as shown at the right. The cap is then screwed on to hold the remainder of the assembly in place. A short section of radiator hose can be slit and trimmed to fit over the reel, or a protecting sleeve can be made from a section of an old inner tube. Many reels come with their own covers.

ADVICE FROM AN ANGLER: If some of your fishing line becomes so tangled that it seems impossible to straighten it out, try using a fishhook for this purpose. Just straighten out the hook and slip a cork over the end. The barb will be ideal for pulling out tangled parts of the line.

THE LINE OF MOST RESISTANCE

Once rod, reel, and lure have done their part to get a fish properly hooked, there is nothing between you and the catch but the line. On that slim, tapering line, often tried far beyond its tested strength by a game fish, depends whether you'll be talking about a fish you caught or "the one that got away."

FLY LINES: Fly line weights are based on the grain weight of the first thirty feet of line. For example, if you have a 7-weight rod, you should be using a 7-weight line. However, if it is a stiff rod and you are casting big air-resistant flies, or you are likely to be casting into strong headwinds, go up a line weight and put an 8-weight line on your 7-weight rod. It'll help punch through the wind.

BAIT-CASTING LINES: Bait-casting lines are graded according to their ability to support dead weights of 8,

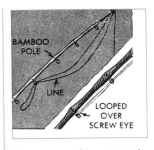

Screw eyes, driven into the joints of a bamboo pole, allow easy variation of line length. The line is fixed to the eye at the pole's end and looped back to one of the eyes in the joints.

10, 12, and higher poundage. In choosing for weight, the fisherman faces the familiar dilemma of fish or sport. A light line will get him more strikes, but it will lose more fish. A heavier line will not be struck as often, but it is much more apt to haul them in. For general use, a 12-pound line is favored by many fishermen. Those in the expert class use from 6- to 9-pound lines for small game fish, and they go as high as 24 pounds in line weight when fishing for the big ones.

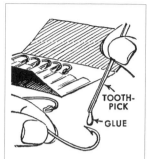

To avoid injuring fingers on a fishhook, put a drop of water-soluble glue on the point of the hook and around the barb. Then the hook can be handled safely. When the hook is placed in the water, the covering will dissolve.

KNOTS AND SPLICES: The best fishing line is subject to a number of causes of deterioration. Friction, mildew, rust, and rot are all deadly enemies of the line. Keep the agate guides of rod and tip smooth so they will not fray the line. The heaviest wear will be found along the first foot from the fly or plug. You can double the strength of the line at this point by forming a twelve-inch loop, tied with a reef knot as shown in "Knots and Ties" on page 73.

ADVICE FROM AN ANGLER: For those who prefer to tie their own trout flies and bass bugs, woodchuck (groundhog) tail hair will serve as an excellent substitute for bucktail hair. It is very similar to bucktail hair and works just as well. To tan wood-chuck tails, first remove the tailbone and tack the tail, flesh side out, in a cool dry place. Then rub salt into the flesh side of the tail. When the tail is dry, pack it in a glass jar along with naphtha flakes or cedar shavings to protect against possible damage by moths.

Splicing a line is a little more trouble, but it will avoid any possible wear or jam when the line passes through guides and tip. A good splice will be stronger than the line itself and almost as smooth. With a razor blade, cut the line ends sharply, then carefully scrape off the line finish for a half inch at each end. After that, using a sharp needle, pick out the individual strands of the braided line. Work a little fly wax in your fingers and rub it onto the strands until they are stiff and sticky. Divide the strands equally and form them into a fork shape. Do the same with the other end of the line. Then join the forks and press down the ends. Get someone to hold the join for you while you begin winding No. 00 silk around the splice, starting at the middle. Wind tightly, one turn at a time, making sure each turn touches the previous one without overlapping. When about six turns from the end of the splice, lay a

Winding a trotline on a reel or spool is done quickly with the aid of a hand drill. The spool is slipped over a tight-fitting bit that is chucked in the drill, and the side handle is clamped in a vise. One hand turns the drill while the other guides the line onto the spool.

loop in the direction of the wind and continue turning over it. When you have reached the finished part of the line, pull the line through the loop, then pull the loop out. The winding thread can be trimmed off flush with the last turn of the splice, leaving an invisible knot underneath the splice. Go back to the middle and repeat the procedure with the other end of the splice. Finish the splice with a single coat of thin varnish.

Chapter 5

HOOK IS BIG "IF" IN FISHING

Consider for a moment the lowly fishhook! Of all the trinkets and doodads in your fishing-tackle kit, it's probably the smallest. It cost you the least. It doesn't look like much. But what's the first part of your tackle to meet the fish eye-to-eye and challenge it to a tussle?

You're right—the hook!

So give the lowly fishhook a second thought, and you'll agree that it's important after all. Whether you're strictly a holiday and vacation fisherman, or a postgraduate angler who really goes at it scientifically, a speaking acquaintance with hook lore will help you land more fish.

ADVICE FROM AN ANGLER: The annoyance of a dangling fishhook while carrying the pole along a creek or river can be avoided by tying a rubber band near the butt of the pole. Tie the rubber so that it must be stretched to engage the hook. In this way, the hook cannot slip out of the band and catch in your clothing.

Casting lead sinkers of the type used for deepwater fishing may be done with an improvised mold made by embedding a burned-out lightbulb in a can of sand. Dampen the sand and pack it around the inverted bulb, but let the sand dry before casting the sinker so that steam will not generate between the sand and the outside of the bulb. After the bulb is filled with molten lead, quickly suspend a hook eye in the lead and let it cool. If many sinkers are to be cast, it is best to make a regular two-part sand mold, using the bulb as a master pattern. If no lightbulb is available, use an eggshell. Break off the pointed end of the egg, remove the contents, set the base of the shell in sand, and proceed as outlined above. Smaller sinkers can be made using an empty thread spool as a mold. Plug one end of the spool, insert a wire in the hole, and fill with molten lead. When this has cooled, the sinker can be pulled out and trimmed to shape with a sharp knife.

HOW A FISHHOOK WORKS

The modern fishhook didn't get its sleek lines and metallurgically foolproof interior through somebody's idle whim! Cavemen invented the hook because they were hungry. The first "hook" actually was a gorge made of flint that the fish could swallow with the bait, but that it could not eject. The cavemen later invented the barb for the same reason. Primitive fishermen tried making hooks of stone, bone, seashells, horn, thorns, and wood. When they learned to use metal, they made better hooks and caught more fish. Most of the features of modern hooks were tried out hundreds or even thousands of years ago.

To know how a fishhook works, you need to know about its various parts. Each part of the hook has a job to do. Each can be designed to do a good job in very special circumstances.

That leaves up to you, the fisherman, the problem of choosing a fishhook with features that will give you advantages in your effort to catch a particular kind and size of fish.

Here are the parts of a hook: the point, which reaches from tip to barb; the bend, giving the hook its curve; the shank, serving as a backbone, and the eye, which guides the leader and line down to the hook.

The scope of a hook—that is, its width between point and shank—is called its throat. And the depth of the hook from throat to bend is called its bite.

MATCHING HOOK TO FISH

Now, there are three qualities that are essential in any hook that lands a fish. The hook must be usable with the bait or lure that the fish will strike. The hook must be able to take hold. And it must be able to keep its hold despite the fish's struggles.

For thousands of years, anglers have been trying to devise a hook that will excel in all three qualities.

But, alas, no such ideal hook exists! Modern tackle manufacturers are still trying to gaff an answer to the problem. Until some

ADVICE FROM AN ANGLER: Fishermen who find it necessary to submerge their hands in cold water to set lines can keep their hands free from chapping during cold weather by rubbing them with olive oil. The coating of oil will keep the hands almost as warm as a pair of gloves.

ADVICE FROM AN ANGLER: Lashed to the end of your fishing rod with thread, a large hook from which the barb has been removed often solves the problem of retrieving your line if it becomes entangled in a tree while you're fishing along wooded shores. To avoid losing your bait when passing through brush, keep both the hook and the bait in a small wide-mouth bottle held on the rod near the handle by a couple of rubber bands. If the bottle is partly filled with water, it will keep the bait from drying out.

inspired fisherman comes up with the solution, you will have to decide which qualities to accent in your hook, and which to sacrifice.

To illustrate: suppose you want to catch a big, husky trout. If you use a big, husky hook, the trout will laugh at you. It's eating mosquitoes today! You must choose a tiny hook to suit the tiny fly, sacrificing holding power.

Or suppose you want to catch a big, savage marlin swordfish (blue marlin), which you know will jitterbug across the waves when it feels the hook. You know it will shake and yank and turn somersaults. The biggest problem is to find a hook that will hold, even at the sacrifice of quick hooking. So you choose a heavy-gauge hook with a curve even closer than a half circle, with a loss in hooking power but a gain in holding power.

Your problem of choosing the proper hook is tougher if you're after more than one kind of fish. The table manners of fish vary as much as their mouths, appetites, and personalities. In size, game fish range from the fingerling trout that nips at gnats to the mighty broadbill that spends its leisure killing whales.

Fish mouths are small like a perch or big like a bass, soft like a young brook trout or bony like a tarpon, smooth like a cobia or toothy like a pike. When choosing your hooks, look for features that will overcome the main problem posed by your particular fish—don't just choose hooks that look rakish.

Hooks vary in hardness and temper. Your best buy in hooks are standard merchandise backed by a reputable maker.

Hooks are made in various sizes of wire: standard, light, or heavy. A light hook weighs less and penetrates more easily, but it is also more likely to rip or spring. A heavy hook penetrates bone and holds better under heavy strain, but it has disadvantages if used on floating lures or with live bait.

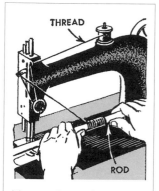

It's easy to wind your own fishing rods. Just mount a spool of silk winding thread on a sewing machine and run the thread through the tension arm, as shown. This holds the silk taut, allowing both hands to be used to rotate the rod.

POINTS

Fishhook points differ in shape and in angle of penetration, which may range from shallow to deep. Needle point, spear point, and hollow point are most popular. The needle point is smooth, thin, and round. When properly made, it is very strong and has excellent penetrating quality. The spear point, usually found on inexpensive hooks, turns slightly outward. The hollow point is a quick hooker for fish with soft mouths.

ADVICE FROM AN ANGLER: Empty film spools make handy temporary storage reels for extra fishlines. The spool flanges are bent up at right angles to provide channels for the line.

ADVICE FROM AN ANGLER: To protect a valuable fly when carrying a casting rod through weeds and brush, you can cut a slit in the side of a hollow rubber ball and slip it over the fly, letting it dangle from the tip of the rod. Another method is to impale the ball on the rod near the grip so that it will always be at hand for the same purpose.

By its angle of penetration, the point enters flesh or bone and enables the hook to take hold. A point that aims slightly away from the hook will penetrate quickly and at a deeper angle. A point that aims parallel with the shank will put maximum pressure on the point of penetration and is best for hard-mouthed fish. A point that aims slightly inward toward the shank loses some of its hooking power but gains in holding power. If turned more than very slightly inward, it loses depth of bite.

BENDS

The bend of a hook not only aims the point, but also gives the hook a bite or hold on which the fishing line can pull. A hook may have a straight bend or an offset bend. A straight-bend hook is on a plane with its point parallel with the shank. An offset-bend hook is twisted at the bend so that the point's aim is askew.

Straight-bend hooks penetrate more nearly in the direction of pull from the fishing line than do offset-bend hooks. They drive harder into bone. The argument for offset hooks is that they are less likely to be withdrawn from a fish's mouth without penetrating. Offset hooks give their best performance in still-bait fishing. Straight-bend hooks are your best bet for moving baits or lures.

SHANKS

The shank of a hook is usually made of rolled steel wire. Sometimes oval wire is used for extra strength. Occasionally, the shank is flattened along the sides of both shank and bend to provide greater strength. A shank may have several slices, or barbs, to help hold soft bait in place.

Shanks of hooks intended for use with lures are frequently humped, to anchor the body of the lure. The longer the shank in proportion to the size of the hook,

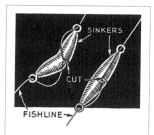

To attach a lead sinker to a fishline so that it can be held at any point without using knots, cut the sinker halfway through so that it can be opened like a hinge.

the shallower will be the bite of the hook. Rather than use an extremely long-shank hook for a streamer lure, use single hooks in tandem. You'll be apt to take more fish that way.

EYES

The eye of a hook may be straight or turned either up or down. Hooks for dry-fly fishing have tapered eyes, for balance and lightness, at a sacrifice of strength. Some eyes are looped or brazed to protect leaders from sharp edges of metal.

ADVICE FROM AN ANGLER: Dry flies can be restored to their original shape by steaming them. This softens the hackle so that it can be forced into place and the wings set at the correct angle.

Where great strength and hard-hooking qualities are needed, as in big-game fishing, the straight eye—also called ringed eye—has been proved best.

ADVICE FROM AN ANGLER: If you break your casting rod while on a fishing trip and are unable to purchase another, you can make one from an ordinary bamboo pole that will serve well for the emergency. Split off three strips, each a half inch wide, from the pole. Cut them to two, three, and five feet in length. The strips are fitted together, concave side down, and bound tightly with electrician's tape. Guides are shaped from short pieces of wire and fastened to the rod with a few turns of tape. Or guides can be cut and shaped from the narrow tip of the pole. The reel is fastened with tape. If no tape is available, a stout cord will serve as a substitute. Spring and taper are provided to the rod by the way in which the strips are joined, the butt end being three ply for two feet, two ply for one foot, and a single strip for the last two feet to the tip end.

Chapter 6

KNOTS AND TIES

Light-tackle fishermen who wet lines in sweet water, from the time of the first hatch of flies in early spring to the close of the season, need to have almost as good a working knowledge of knot tying as did the old-time sailors. Although the history of the development of knot tying is in many instances not definitively known, it is fairly certain that many of the knots now used by fly fishermen were developed in earlier days by good marlinespike seamen and by fishing sailors.

Experienced freshwater fishermen usually choose only the types of knots that seem best suited to their purpose and use these regularly for everyday fishing needs. Anyone can learn to tie any knot, from the simplest to the most complicated, but some knots require much more practice than others before the process of tying them can be clearly established in the mind. As a rule, fishermen do not use involved knots, as these are usually bulky even when cinched up tightly. Such knots offer considerable resistance to movement through the water, leave a trail of bubbles underwater, and form a wake when on the surface. These features are objectionable to most fishermen. Among the knots

For joining the ends of leaders, the fisherman's bend is perhaps the simplest of barrel-knot ties

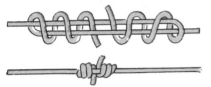

Another variation of the fisherman's bend which is preferred by some anglers for artificial leaders

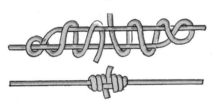

A third variation with turns made in the opposite direction. Work out the slack gradually

The blood-knot bend builds up a neat, smooth tie

approved by nearly all fly fishermen for joining lines to leaders are the single sheet bend, the reef and figure-of-eight knots, the overhand jam knot, and the tiller or slipped hitch. Some anglers do not approve of the overhand jam knot, but it will be noted that when the tie is properly finished it makes a neat, reliable knot that is no larger than the leader loop. It can be whipped through a quiet pool with practically no disturbance of the water. The simplest and quickest, perhaps, of all these knots to tie and untie is the single sheet bend; of course, the neatest and smoothest one of all is the reef knot with the free end seized to the standing part.

For joining the ends of leaders when building up a long, single leader, the details above on this page show several variations of the barrel-knot bend, or double fisherman's bend, as it is often called. The knot in the lower detail is

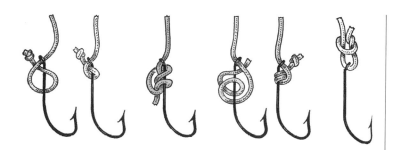

Of the four fishhook ties, left to right above, the first two are the familiar single sheet bend with an overhand knot in the end of the line. The next is the round-turn fishhook tie before drawing up. Following this comes the double sheet bend, shown loose and drawn up, and finally an application of the overhand knot.

perhaps more properly called the blood-knot bend. The trick in tying these bends is not in the formation of the knot, which is comparatively simple, but in working out the slack and drawing up the turns to make a smooth tie. This is especially true of the fishhook ties shown in this chapter. All of these are detailed either loose or partly drawn up. None are shown cinched up tight, as they would be when in use. One of the most popular knots for attaching lines to hooks is the familiar single sheet bend. An overhand knot tied in the end of the line prevents slipping or pulling out. Some fishermen prefer the double sheet bend for attaching fine lines to small hooks. Other knots in the series shown are used extensively by fishermen when building up heavy tackle. Although it's not shown in all details above, many fishermen tie an overhand knot in the end of the line as a regular practice when tying either lines or leaders to hooks. It should be noted, of course, that most of the fishhook ties are used by fishermen for tying both lines and leader to hooks or eyed flies.

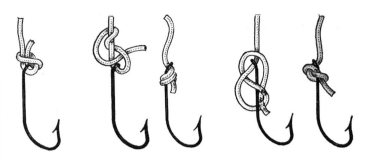

Left to right, the first detail shows the sliding overhand knot pulled up to the eye of the hook. The next two details show the wedge tie loose and drawn up, the knot being slipped over the turned-down eye of the hook. The last two details show a figure-of-eight knot, in common use among fishermen. Note that the knot is drawn up below the eye.

The turle knot, shown in the first three details below, is considered by many anglers to be the best ever developed for tying either lines or leaders to hooks and leaders to flies. As you can see by a study of the knot formation, it is simply a sliding overhand knot, that knot being tied on the standing part after

Left to right below, the first two details show how the turle knot tie is used to attach the line to the hook. The third detail shows the application of this knot when joining eyed flies to line or leader. The fourth detail is a twisted tie that is especially suitable for attaching eyed flies to artificial leaders. Work the turns tight.

the line has been passed through the eye of the hook. The loop is then passed over the hook or fly and snugged up against the eye. Hold the overhand knot tightly between the thumb and forefinger when pulling up the loop. Simplicity is the feature of the twisted tie shown in the fourth, or right-hand, detail below on the preceding page. It is quite similar to the timber hitch and holds securely when the turns are carefully worked down to the eye of the hook or fly. The three details at the bottom of this page show two methods of attaching a dropper fly. Two overhand knots are tied side by side. Then the knotted end of the dropper is inserted between the standing parts, as shown. The overhand knots are then worked up against the dropper and drawn tight. In the left detail below, the knots are not shown fully drawn up. In the right-hand detail below, a barrel knot is tied on the line to prevent slipping, and the dropper is attached by means of an angler's loop. In certain applications, the name of the knot is determined to some extent by variations in common use. An example is the ordinary slipknot. It is also referred to as the jam knot and the sliding overhand knot—but, of course, it consists of essentially the same formation. The same is true of certain other knots in various applications.

Left to right below are two methods of attaching a dropper fly. In the first detail, overhand knots are tied side by side, or back to back, as shown. Then the knots are drawn up over the knotted end of the dropper, as in the center detail. The right-hand illustration shows a barrel knot combined with an angler's loop.

TYING LINES TO LEADERS

This knot is known quite generally to fishermen as the single tie or single sheet bend. The detail above shows a common way of starting the tie.

Here is the same tie with the formation of the knot completed by passing the line under the standing part before drawing the knot tight.

Drawn up, the single tie looks something like this. It cinches up lightly under a moderate strain and is easy to untie after slacking off.

Here again is the single sheet bend with an overhand knot on the end of the line. In drawing up, the overhand knot is worked down to the bend.

Somewhat simpler than the sheet bend, the reef knot cinches tightly and holds fast, but when tension is released the loop can be slacked off.

The popular figure-of-eight knot can be used to attach the fly to the leader or the leader to the line. This is a simple, reliable fly fisherman's tie.

The first stage in tying the overhand jam knot. Here it is simply a slipknot, with the overhand knot tied around the standing part of the line.

The slipknot becomes a sheet bend when worked down over the end of the leader loop and tightened. Many fly fishermen prefer this neat tie.

Sometimes called the tiller knot, the slipped hitch is especially desirable because it is easy to untie: Just slack off and pull on the free end.

This is the reef knot again, but with the end of the line seized to the standing part. It's smoother even than the jam knot, as there are no dangling ends.

Chapter 7

GET A BOAT
YOU CAN ROCK

There comes a time in the life of every veteran fisherman when he wants his own boat. The ones he begs, borrows, or hires at an exorbitant rate after he gets to his favorite fishing grounds never seem satisfactory for the purpose. If flat-bottomed, the care given their seams often has been so negligible as to have him standing ankle-deep in water at the end of a fishing day. If they are keel-bottomed craft, such boats are usually too large, or not too steady for the moving about and casting that a fisherman must do from a boat.

Thus, you may want to buy or make your own boat. Whichever course you adopt, you must first decide on the type of boat that you need. Remember that you want a boat primarily for fishing—therefore, factors that might seem to be a drawback in boats for

ADVICE FROM AN ANGLER: To help avoid slipping off of the seat when pulling on the oars of a heavy boat, cover the seat with a rubber stair tread. The curved edge of the tread engages the back edge of the seat so that it will not slide forward under the movement of the boatman.

general use will be excellent for your purpose.

First of all, your boat must fit the kind of fishing you do. If you fish calm lakes or broad, still rivers, you'll want a flat-bottomed boat. Best of all for these waters is the pram-type dinghy or skiff, with both ends squared. This makes it possible to fish from either end of the boat with the same easy balance.

By hinging the seat of your rowboat and notching the cross brace underneath it to take the oars, you can provide a place to lock them. One end of the seat is fitted with a hasp and padlock.

Choppy lakes or swift rivers will call for a V-bottomed boat. Built with a raised bow and equipped with a freeboard that can be raised or lowered easily, such a boat will provide almost the steadiness of the flat-bottomed craft.

Size is an important factor in choosing a fishing boat. Don't get or build it too big. Two is about the limit in number of persons who can fish together from a boat, and a twelve- or fourteen-foot boat is the outside size for most fishing. If you are going to pack your boat on top of your car, a ten- or even eight-foot craft will be lighter and easier to handle.

The material isn't important, as long as it makes for a light, rugged, and watertight boat. Good fishing can be had from the conventional planked wood boat, or from those made of sheet plywood, metal, or plastic. Aluminum, stainless steel, and magnesium have been used in highly successful small boats.

In shopping for a new or used boat, there are several things to guard against. Poor workmanship in a boat is probably best detected at the joints of planks, ribs, keel, stem, and transom. These should fit closely, and they should be joined with screws as well as nails. Check the paint job for rough places and an uneven spread of the coat. Make sure some preservative has been applied against both wet and dry rot.

You can carry your casting rod safely in a rowboat, where it will be out of the way yet handy for instant use, by mounting a couple of wooden blocks inside the boat just below the gunwale. Shallow holes or sockets are bored in the blocks, after which they are spaced and attached securely so that the handle and top of the rod slip into them when they are slightly bowed against the side of the boat.

For a fishing boat, you'll want wide, solid seats—if there is a lot of "give" in the seats, they will not stand up under a heavy load in rough water. You'll also want plenty of legroom. This should be checked by getting in the boat to see whether it will be comfortable for both rowing and fishing movements. There should be at least one roomy locker for your fishing tackle and other gear.

To keep your fishing tackle on the boat seat beside you, just saw two notches in the front and rear edges of the seat to take stout rubber bands. Then set the box on the seat and slip the bands up over the ends; the box will be held securely.

If you're going to put an outboard motor on your boat, remember that you are going fishing—not racing. Choose the lightest motor that can handle your boat, somewhere between

ADVICE FROM AN ANGLER: Two watertight bulkheads under the middle seat of a rowboat provide a bait well where the water is always cool and fresh. Paint with white lead and linseed oil and caulk with marine glue.

1½ and 5 hp. Make sure it will idle efficiently, so as to give you a dependable and uniform slow speed for trolling—not all outboard motors will do this successfully.

If you are fairly handy with tools, you can make your own boat. The amateur cannot be warned too strongly, however, to study the plans and follow them carefully. A mistake in boatbuilding

A rowboat seat is more comfortable if it has a folding backrest like the one shown here, which clamps to the regular seat on the boat. A standard-size life preserver cushion may be used for the back and for the seat, and canvas may be stretched over the back.

is expensive and oftentimes hard to detect and rectify. There are many boat plans and blueprints available. *Popular Mechanics* has a book on boatbuilding, as well as a number of good blueprints.

Your boat will need very little repair if it is taken from the water and stored at the end of every season. Boats that are tied up in the water become waterlogged and rot very quickly. When the paint becomes chalky and shows signs of wear, sandpaper the boat and give it a new coat of good-quality paint. Lead and oil paint can be used for the part above the waterline. Copper bottom paint should be applied below the waterline.

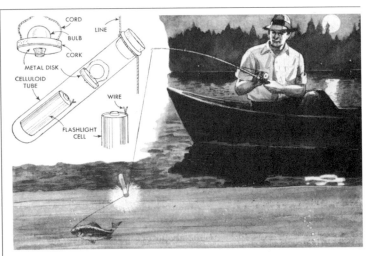

Fishermen who work the ponds, lakes, and river backwaters where night fishing for catfish, bullheads, and other night feeders is permitted will appreciate this illuminating fishing float, which flashes a light at the slightest nibble. It consists of a penlight cell that slides inside a glass or celluloid tube to make contact with a bulb when the tube is tipped.

Chapter 8

RETRIEVING LOST LURES, LINES, AND RODS

Heartbreaking is the word for it when a long-cherished lure gets snagged in the weeds, then lost on the bottom when your clumsy attempts to free it break the line. Frustration is a mild term for the feeling you get when your cast gets no farther than the backswing, and an expensive fly is caught and broken in the branches of a tree. In deep water, not only the lure but also a goodly portion of expensive line can be lost when a lure is snagged.

Since hooks are scientifically designed to catch and hold, it's not surprising that a lot of trouble can

ADVICE FROM AN ANGLER: If your line should break and leave your lure stranded on the bottom, it is often possible to recover it by using a burlap bag filled with grass or leaves. A few stones are placed in the sack on top of the grass or leaves to make it sink. The bag is pulled along the bottom of the stream or lake at the approximate position of the lost lure. Then, as the bag is moved across the lure, the hooks will engage the meshes of the sack and can be pulled free.

Here is a handy gadget for use when your fly, leader, and maybe a yard or two of line are wound irretrievably around a small twig somewhere high out of reach. The tool is simply a piece of 1/32-inch steel with a V-shaped cutting edge ground razor sharp. One side of the cutter is slotted so that it can be hooked over the rod tip and raised to the offending twig, as indicated. Then, after disengaging the rod, you can give the cord a strong pull that will bring down the twig and line.

develop from weeds, submerged underbrush, and logs, and, for the fly fisherman, from overhanging bushes and trees.

When your line is snagged underwater, it's a good idea to remember that hooks were designed to hold a fish that's running away from you. Your efforts to free a snagged hook, therefore, should be from some other direction. Move around to the opposite side from where you were fishing, if possible, or at least well to the side. If you can get directly over the snagged lure and exert a slow, steady pull, that's even better. And there are several old fisherman's tricks you can use to meet or avoid such emergencies.

If you are fishing in water where the bottom is rocky, or there are other obstructions that may snag your tackle, try the following method: attach the sinker below the hooks, to keep the hooks off the bottom and thus reduce the chances of snagging, and partly sever the line between the sinker and the hooks. Then, if the sinker catches on something, a jerk will break the line so that only the sinker is lost.

A heavy coil spring with a strong cord attached will be found useful in loosening fishhooks that have become snagged on a submerged log or entangled in debris. The spring is slipped over the fishing line and allowed to slide down to the snagged hook. Often, the force of the dropping spring will be enough to dislodge the hook. If not, pulling on the cord from one side will allow the spring to act as a lever and disengage the hook.

A small ball of carpenters' chalk line or a similar cord is carried by many fishermen on every angling expedition. If a line is nagged, tie a small rock to the end of the cord. Just above the rock, tie a ten-inch loop. Then draw your snagged line tight and set your fishing rod in the bank to hold the line taut. Throw the rock weight over the spot where the hook is tangled. By manipulating the cord, you can usually manage to engage the snagged tackle in the loop and pull it loose.

An underwater flashlight, for locating fishing tackle and other objects dropped from a pier or boat into shallow water at night, can be made by sealing a small flashlight in a fruit jar fitted with a rubber ring. To do this, turn the light on and place it in the

jar so that the beam is directed through the bottom. After making sure the rubber lid washer is in good condition, to prevent water from seeping into the jar, screw the lid on tightly. Then hold the jar underwater, and the flashlight should provide enough illumination to permit locating the item.

When a tackle box slides off the boat's seat into the water, that doesn't mean the end of the fishing trip and the loss of tackle—if the box is equipped with a life preserver like the one shown above. To make it, cut down an inner tube so that it will fit snugly about the box when inflated. Cement rubber strips to the corners of

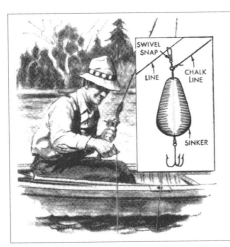

By using a fairly large bell-type sinker rigged with a treble hook and a swivel snap to attach it to the fishing line, plugs or spoons that have become snagged often can be worked free. A chalk line is tied to the swivel snap to manipulate the sinker. To release a lure, get above the snag and bob with the sinker.

the box to provide a grip for the tube. To make it easier to inflate the preserver, remove the valve core and use an airtight cap on the valve stem.

When a fishing rod is accidentally dropped in the water, chances are it will never be recovered unless a marker or buoy is floated over the place where it disappeared. A marker can be

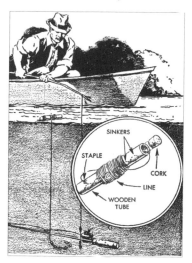

made from a wooden tube, such as a piece of bamboo or alder. One end of the tube is plugged and sealed, and a cork is fitted in the other end. A length of fishing line, stapled to the tube, is weighted at one end with sinkers, which can be kept in the tube when not in use. When a rod is dropped, the weighted line is lowered to mark the place, and the tube will float on the water while preparations are being made for retrieving the rod.

A small cork placed on a fishing line between the lead sinker and the hook will keep the bait off the bottom of a lake or river and prevent it from snagging. The cork should be large enough to float the baited hook, but too small to lift the sinker. A cork of the proper size used in this manner will not interfere greatly with ordinary casting.

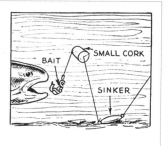

Chapter 9

WHEN AND WHERE TO FISH

There are about as many ideas as to where and when to fish as there are fishermen. These ideas range from those in the "old wives' tale" class to the scientific findings of ichthyologists and the practical observations of veteran fishermen. There are some sound rules, all with exceptions to prove them.

One primary rule is to ask for advice in the particular locality. Even the professional fishermen, proud of their own fish lore, make a practice of this. Ask resident fishermen where the fish are and what sort of lures they are taking.

Some spots in every lake or stream are better than others that look just as good. Often the best way to fish one lake is a poor way to fish another. There's one chain of lakes, almost side by side and fed by the same

ADVICE FROM AN ANGLER: Fishhooks can be kept from getting tangled and scattered around by just stringing them on a safety pin. Pins of various sizes may be used in proportion to the number and size of hooks carried, which can be taken off one at a time as they are needed.

stream, that takes bait fishing in the upper lake, fly casting in the middle lake, and trolling in the third for best results. Different water conditions and feed account for this.

A good fisherman makes a careful, quiet approach to the spot that he hopes to fish. He watches for fish and tries to see what they are feeding on. If none are active, he looks for them among rocks, underbrush, logs, and branches. Generally, he uses a plug or spinner early in the season and changes to a fly when warm weather heats the water and brings the fish to the surface. Bugs and flies hatch onto the surface of the water in warm weather, and the fish rise to this feed.

The good fisherman uses the lightest leader and smallest hook practicable. They will catch more fish than heavy

To carry small fishhooks where they will be handy at all times, slip the barb points under a pencil eraser of the slip-on type. When clipped to your pocket, the pencil holds the hooks safely.

tackle that the fish can readily identify as strange to its waters. The good fisherman remembers that fish are timid. Vibrations caused when you stumble over a rock or when you row a boat carelessly will scare fish away. Chunking a bait or fly into the water with a splash will frighten most of them. So does your shadow on the water, or your active movements if you are standing against the sky. Try to stand with your back to the sun, far enough from the water so that your shadow is on the bank.

WEATHER

Fish apparently are hungrier, or at least they bite better, in spring and fall than in midsummer. Generally, any mild, sunny day that we associate with the phrase "nice weather" is good for fishing. However, many fish bite vigorously on a cloudy, overcast day, particularly during the few hours before a rain. After a thunderstorm or a very heavy rain, the water is usually too rough and cloudy for good fishing, and usually it will have to settle for a few days before the fish resume feeding. Most fish head for deep water at the first signs of thunder or lightning, and they stay there until the weather clears. Wind direction is not as important as some fishermen believe. But the force of the wind has a definite bearing on the way fish will bite. A slight breeze that just ruffles the surface of the water is ideal. Heavier winds will find the fish on the lee shore or in the protection of bays, coves, and lagoons.

TIME

Most fish are night feeders. This would seem to be the ideal time to fish for them, except that it is extremely difficult to handle and land a game fish when you can't see it. You have to compromise and follow when the fish are just starting to get hungry and just before they stop feeding. The best times, therefore, will be between sunrise and midmorning, and from about two hours before sunset until the last light fades. Night casting is practiced by many bass fishermen, even though it is difficult to land the fish in the dark. This is the time when the fish, especially bass, come out of the deep water and bask in the shallows. Choose a heavy rod, since the fish are likely to be larger than those hooked in daytime fishing. Bright-colored lures or, better still, luminous ones are chosen—not for the benefit of the fish, but to make them easier for the caster to follow. Keep your casts short—longer ones will tend to snag or backlash, and you'll have trouble untangling them in the dark. Be as quiet as you can, since the fish expect it to be quiet at night. If you land a fish or have a noisy strike, leave the spot for a while and fish somewhere else.

TEMPERATURE

More important than weather or time is the temperature of the water. That is because each species of fish has a certain water temperature in which it lives and thrives best. It may go out of this temperature range in search of food or to flee from enemies, but it will always return when hunger or fear have gone. For instance, in a body of water containing smallmouth and largemouth bass, there will rarely be mixed schools of fish. Smallmouth bass like a temperature as close to 67 degrees as possible, while largemouth bass prefer a water temperature of about 70 degrees or slightly above. The smallmouths, therefore, will be found at a deeper level than the largemouths in summer, when the deepest water is coolest. In winter, however, the deepest water is warmest, and the two

ADVICE FROM AN ANGLER: Fishermen who like to use a float for all types of fishing, but often find that it rides too high in the water, especially when a sinker isn't used on the line, can weight the float with No. 4 shot to make it ride in the water as desired. If the float is made of cork, the shot can be pushed into it near the lower end with a tapered matchstick. When a wood float is used, tiny holes can be bored into it and the shot forced into them in the same way. After you insert the shot, a daub of paint will keep water from entering the holes.

To relieve eyestrain caused by looking through the mesh of a head net for long periods of time, one fisherman mounted a rectangular piece of transparent plastic in the netting directly in front of his eyes. This permits clear vision while still giving the head protection from insects. An opening is cut in the netting, and the window is cemented directly to the edges of the netting.

kinds of fish may reverse their positions to be in water nearest the temperature they prefer.

Brook trout like much colder water than bass. You'll find them active in temperatures between 50 and 65 degrees. Lake trout like it even colder, between 40 and 50 degrees. The warmer waters, between 70 and 80 degrees, are the happy hunting grounds of pike, pickerel, and muskellunge. You can buy an inexpensive fishing thermometer, keyed to an accompanying chart of fish temperature preferences, which will help you find the fishing level on most occasions.

COVER

Most of the time, fish lie where they can simultaneously find food and protection from their enemies. Warm-water fish, therefore, will generally be around weed beds or beneath overhanging trees and brush along the shore of a lake or stream. Cold-water fish, on the other hand, will be lying around rocks and ledges offshore or in the center of the body of water. Your bait or lure should be dropped as close to natural cover as possible without fouling the tackle.

CHUMMING

A method of attracting fish to a certain spot is to chum or bait a certain part of the lake or stream. The area can be marked off with stakes or buoys, or by noting landmarks. Ground fish, pork, dead minnows, worms, and other fish foods are scattered over the area. There are two drawbacks to chumming. One is that a number of small fish are attracted as well as the big ones, and you're likely to be as busy throwing them back as you are taking them in. Another is the fact that, unless you're desperate for fish, the method is not regarded as sportsmanlike.

When tying a hook to your fishline, do it as shown in the lower detail, and then you can remove it easily when necessary. In addition, if moving from one fishing spot to another makes it necessary to add another sinker, you can do it, as shown in the upper detail, without cutting the line.

TROLLING

In stormy weather, or on exceptionally hot and muggy days, the fish will go so deep that casting and bait fishing from a pole become a waste of time. Trolling, or drifting live bait on a long line from a boat, is the answer to such fishing conditions. The important thing in trolling is to keep your bait about a foot from the bottom. This can be done by putting a sinker on the end of the line, with the

ADVICE FROM AN ANGLER: An empty matchbook may be converted readily to serve as a holder for carrying extra fish-hooks safely; as it is flat, it takes less space in your pocket than a cork. The hooks are inserted in slits cut in the book, so that they are completely covered when the book is closed. As the eyes are pushed into the stapled portion, there is little chance of the hooks dropping out of the holder. Use the scratching portion of the book to sharpen hooks. The abrasive surface will restore the points quickly.

baited hook a foot above it. Minnows, frogs, and pork chunks are the likeliest baits for trolling. Row the boat slowly and steadily, or let it drift if there is sufficient current. Don't pull up on nibbles—with that length of line out, you'll have to wait until the fish is securely hooked before attempting to bring it in.

Use several floats on your line when still-fishing from the bank of a lake or stream. They will support the line on the surface of the water, instead of allowing it to sink and to tend to pull the hook close to the bank. When the line is kept on the surface of the water, minnows playing with the bait cannot tangle the hook into it, which they often do if it sinks.

FLOATS

LAKES

Whenever you visit a strange lake, devote the first evening to silent watching. Find a vantage point that gives a view of the entire surface, then just sit and watch from shortly before sundown until after dark. Watch for feeding fish. Pay little attention to the occasional lone fish that jumps clear out of the water near the middle of the lake. Instead, watch for those boils on the surface that reveal the location of several feeding fish. If they occur repeatedly, that spot is sure to be a good place to fish. Mark it for the next day's fishing.

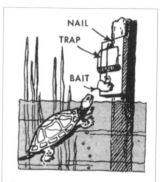

Spring-type rat traps set on posts in shallow water and baited with raw meat or chicken heads will rid a pond or lake of turtles. Nail the trap to the post with the bait slightly above the water level.

The signs you see will depend on the kind of fish and on the type of food they are taking. Boils at the surface mean the fish are taking insects of some kind. Long V-shaped ripples indicate fish are chasing minnows, while shorter ones mean that frogs are the bait.

Note the time the feeding begins, and be there ready for

ADVICE FROM AN ANGLER: To troll at very low speeds with an outboard motorboat, use a motor with full reverse and operate the boat stern first. The drag of the transom will maintain as low a speed as you wish. Be sure to stay away from shoal water, as the motor cannot be tilted in this reversed position. Alternatively, use a small electric motor.

action the following evening. Usually just a few minutes' inspection of the surface will reveal the type of food the fish are taking. Match it as nearly as possible with an artificial lure, or the real thing if you can, and you should begin taking fish.

When the surface signs fail, or when for any reason you can't make it the night before, you will have to go and hunt for fish. The first thing to do is to make an inspection of the shoreline. I like to do this from a boat driven by an outboard motor, cruising slowly, close to shore all the way around the lake. Look for stumps, logs, weed patches, overhanging grassy banks, mouths of streams entering the lake, clear channels through weed beds, and open pockets in the weeds. Watch for underwater reefs and ledges and for sandy bars that drop off into deeper water. Small islands in the lake are always good.

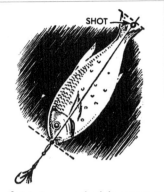

If it is inconvenient to carry a ruler for measuring the fish you catch to see if they are of legal size, just attach an extra split-shot sinker to the line. Space it a distance from the regular sinker equal to the length of fish that you can legally keep. Then it is just a matter of measuring the length of a fish between the two sinkers to determine whether or not it can legally be kept.

Probably the best spot in a lake to catch fish is where a stream enters through a heavy growth of reeds or weeds. There are always fish moving around the edges of weed beds, feeding on bugs, hellgrammites, frogs, or minnows. Where a stream carries additional food into the lake near the weeds, the attractions to the hungry fish are even greater.

During midday, when the fish are resting, you will work a little harder to get results. Cast into open pockets in the weeds, among logs, in deep holes near rocks, or under bushes. Sometimes it requires several casts to arouse a resting fish to the striking point. Don't give up too easily. Make repeated casts to the same spot before moving on.

STREAMS

Many fishermen make two mistakes in stream fishing. First, they go pounding up to the very bank of any pool they intend to fish, unwittingly scaring every fish in the pool. Fish can't hear normal sounds made above water—loud talking won't disturb them—but walking or wading sends warning tremors through the ground and water that will put the fish down and stop their feeding for some time. This is especially true in small streams running through flatlands and meadows.

The average angler's second mistake is tramping from pool to pool, ignoring the shallow riffles between. The pools are the obvious places and apt to be overfished. Frequently, you can put a good fish or two in the creel by floating a lure down through the riffles from a concealed position.

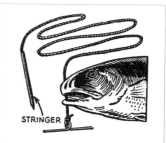

STRINGER

If you have had trouble with fish dying on a stringer, it is possible they were drowned by stringing them through the gills. On some kinds of fish, this prevents normal operation of the mouth and gills, and the fish soon die. To avoid this, run the stringer through the fish's lips, as indicated. When this is done, the fish can operate its gills and mouth in the normal way.

Most of our better fishing streams fall into one of two classifications: fast-moving streams flowing through mountains and heavily wooded terrain, or slower streams flowing through open, flat country. Let's take a look at both types of water for the signs that will locate fish.

In fast streams, look for patches of quiet water where fish can rest without fighting the current. Such spots will occur behind large rocks, jams, fallen trees, and sunken logs, in eddies where the current sweeps around outcropping boulders, and under banks where the stream bends. Any place where you see a patch of dark water in the midst of churning riffles is a good place for a lure.

Places where trees have fallen into the stream make excellent feeding spots. Study the conditions here for a few minutes to determine the best approach for your lure. If the tree trunk is submerged a few inches with water flowing over it, put the lure

This combination balance scale and ruler is made for the fisherman who wants to weigh his catch on the spot, and he can also use it to measure fish of a doubtful legal length. A one-foot ruler made of hardwood will serve as the beam. The end that has

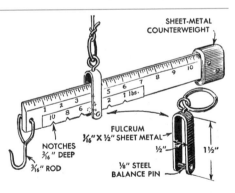

the 12-inch mark should be counterweighted with enough lead or sheet metal so the scale will balance when a 1-pound weight is hung from a metal hook, made from a ³⁄₁₆-inch rod, attached to the opposite end. The fulcrum is made of sheet metal with a steel balance pin. A steel rod or a non-rusting material can be used to form the scale hook. The location of the notches is determined by using weights from a regular scale.

A good artificial bait for bluegills, crappies, or sunfish can be made from several white or natural-color rubber bands and a short-shanked hook. Insert rubber bands through the eye of the hook (detail 1), and trim off their ends, as in detail 2. Then tie the rubber bands to the shank of the hook, just below the eye, with red silk thread, as in detail 3. The bands impart a crawling motion to the bait. You can increase the attraction of the lure by attaching an o-size spinner above the bait.

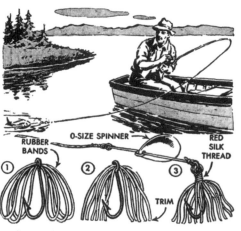

in a few feet above that spot. Use no weight, so that the lure will float naturally over the tree into the quieter water beyond.

The vee at the lower end of small islands in fast streams is frequently good for a fish or two. Cast the lure into fast water a little above where it swirls into the eddy. That brings the lure to the waiting fish in exactly the manner it expects food to arrive. If you don't get a fish from one side of the vee, cross the stream and try from the other side. Never make a cast so that the leader falls across quiet water.

If you have to wade to get into place, approach from one side rather than from above. In fast water of this nature, the fish isn't likely to see you, and you can get quite close if you avoid dislodging rocks directly above the fish.

Fishing a meandering stream in open meadowland involves an entirely different technique. In general, you should look for the same signs, but your whole approach becomes vastly more important. There is seldom any cover in back of you to hide your silhouette. The smooth surface allows the fish to see more clearly—and, instinctively knowing that they in turn can be seen more clearly, they dart for cover at the slightest movement.

Always approach a meadow stream cautiously from one side. Study the spot you want to fish from a distance to determine the flow, whether there are undercuts along the banks, and the point where you should make the

In order to keep your fishing plugs ready for instant selection, transfer them from the tackle box to a notched trough on bamboo, tacked to one side of the boat. In this way, several plugs can be kept in order.

cast. Now approach from one side, making sure your figure does not loom up suddenly. If necessary, traverse the last few feet on your knees. If there are shrubs, weeds, or high grass along the stream's edge, stay behind them and make a blind cast.

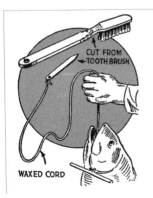

Instead of using a piece of wire or wood on your fish stringer, get an old toothbrush and use it for that purpose. Just cut off the bristle portion of the brush and point one end of the handle. Usually the other end is already drilled, so the stringer can be tied to it. This makes a strong, serviceable point for the end of the stringer, which will be rustproof.

Rise up just enough to enable you to watch through the leaves as your lure floats into the desired spot. If there is no strike, lift the lure gently from the water for the next cast. Never jerk a lure from quiet waters.

Along these open streams, look for deep pools and undercuts in grassy banks. Ride the lure into them without fuss from above. Work from one side, well back, never showing yourself at the stream's edge with the clear sky behind you. It is usually best to approach the water with the sun at your back, providing that your shadow does not fall directly on the water. Fish, like people, have difficulty looking into the sun. For the same reason, try to cast the lure to float on the sun side of where you believe the fish to be. They are more likely to mistake an artificial lure for the real thing and less likely to detect the leader when looking in the direction of the sun.

WADING

In these days of overfished waters, it is the deep-wading angler who catches the most and largest fish. The "big ones"—trout, bass, and other game species—are wise and

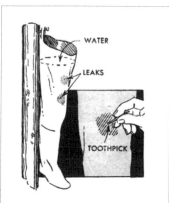

Small holes in hip boots may be easily located by turning the boot inside out, hanging it on a nail, and filling it with water. The leak will show as a damp spot on the fabric. This is marked for repair by inserting a round toothpick into the hole. Small leaks in rubber boots can be sealed by cementing pieces of rubber band in the holes. Work some rubber cement into the hole and stuff with short lengths of rubber bands. Clip the ends when the patch dries.

shy, and they stay far out from the shore-bound caster. Reach them through proper wading methods, and you will discover new thrills in fishing.

In large streams, the experienced angler can cover a great deal more water than from shore and fish it better. In lake fishing, he is able to wade out on the sloping gravel bar or rocky shelf and cast his fly or bait into the deeper waters that are denied to the shore fisherman.

Hip boots are conventional equipment for wading, but they have their limitations. They serve only for shallow water, and their soles may slip dangerously on rocks. But if you use good waders, coming above the waist or even up to the armpits, a new area of a broad river or of typical bass or trout lake will be open to you.

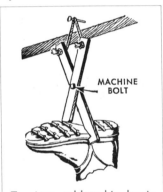

MACHINE BOLT

Buy waders that are long enough in the leg to permit comfortable squatting when going through fences, over logs, and through bush. A drawstring pulled tight at the top will prevent leakage of water when you go in too deep. By the same token, the imprisoned air will actually float you if you should step into a deep hole. Thus, properly worn, waders are not dangerous, as is sometimes supposed. They are far safer than hip boots. It is the weight of water inside wading equipment that can drag down an unwary angler.

To store rubber hip boots without danger of their becoming cracked at the knees, suspend them from wood tongs notched at one end, to grip the sole of the boot, and joined at the center with a machine bolt. A length of cord fastened between the ends causes the tongs to grip tightly.

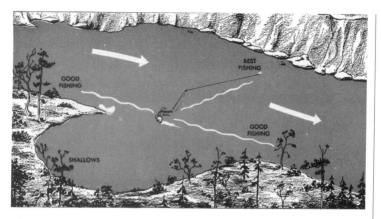

The diagram shows several good fishing spots for the wader.

The wading angler enjoys many advantages over the fellow who must fish from shore. By wading out perhaps 40 feet in a broad stream where his back is clear, he can send his offering another 60 to 80 feet, or a total of 120 feet from shore—more than twice the distance possible when shore fishing. And he can turn at right angles to fish up or down the river or lake, past a bushy point or rocky cliff, in water impossible to reach from a shore position.

Chapter 10

FLY CASTING

By Joe Godfrey Jr., *International authority on fishing, founder and executive secretary of the Sportsman's Club of America, founder of the Fishing Hall of Fame, and author of several well-known books on fishing.*

This is a story of just average fishermen who, because of their choice of proper flies and fly-rod equipment, as well as their knowledge of where to go and what times of day and evening to fish, must hide behind trees when tying flies to their leaders.

Because catching trout, bass, pike, panfish, walleyes, salmon, landlocked salmon, bonefish, snook, tarpon, jack crevalle, steelhead, and sea trout with fly-fishing gear is so much fun and fly casting is so easy to learn, this sport is gaining tremendously in popularity throughout the sports world.

With about half an hour of coaching, you can learn enough about fly casting to catch numerous species of freshwater and saltwater game fish—but it will take many years of conversing with the expert anglers before you will be able to talk as they do. It takes years of rubbing elbows with them at their clubs and in their streams to understand their "fly talk"—but you won't need this until later in life, when sittin' beats wadin'.

What counts most is that electric thrill that goes up the rod through the palm of your hand, up your arm, and into your heart when a fish is on your fly. And another important factor is that friendly feeling you build up inside for those with whom you fish.

There are millions of fishermen who prefer catching fish with a fly rod because it's the sporty way. The purist casts nothing but a dry fly that floats on the surface of the water. Next comes the angler who first tries it dry, then wet to get the big ones that are deeper during the middle of the day, and then dry again for the evening fishing. Third in line is the guy who mostly has in mind that he does not want to visit the commercial fish market on his way home. He goes to the stream, lake, or bay fully equipped with dry and wet flies, streamers, nymphs, cork-bodied bugs, spinners, midget spoons, tiny plugs, and worms. The last type of fisherman is there for the sport itself, and for the thrill that comes along with hooking "the big one." He is a subscriber to the catch-and-release philosophy, and he takes pride in the knowledge that he is leaving his fishing site just as he found it.

There are many ways of catching fish, but here is a list of the most highly approved methods:

1. Dry-fly fishing
2. Wet-fly fishing
3. Spinner fishing
4. Spinning
5. Bait casting
6. Trolling with artificials
7. Trolling with bait
8. Bobber fishing with bait
9. Set-line fishing
10. Net fishing

You may catch more fish if you reverse the above list, but it won't be as much fun.

The sport of fly fishing has in its fold at least two kinds of persons: the serious-minded angler, who insists that he did not "catch" an Atlantic salmon, but rather he "killed" it, and he will further tell you why he used a No. 1 Jock Scott fly and on what the salmon were "feeding"; and the average or absentminded fisherman, who "caught" a salmon on something he thinks was a Dusty Miller fly, but he doesn't remember why he selected it or what size it was, and he doesn't care much what the fish were "eating" at the time. He does remember having a heap of fun taking this fish.

If, in your travels, you hear anglers telling of their catches (I use "catch" instead of "kill" on purpose; these fish were thrown back), and if some of the stories sound exaggerated, go along with these fishermen as though you believed their yarns—provided you reserve your own stories for last.

Truth is something more or less unknown in fishing circles— because who wants to listen to a little-fish story?

But what part of this fishing business is truthful, and where do we draw the line? Well, here it is, and you can count on this information just as you can be sure that fresh-caught walleye is good eating.

- It is true that fish grow a lot faster after they are taken from the water.

- It is not true that fishing is a delusion entirely surrounded by liars in old clothes.

- It is true that fishing is a disease for which there is no cure.

- It is true that opening day is the time when an avalanche of anglers crowds our streams in search of a few scared trout.

- It is true that a creel is a wicker basket in which the fly angler carries a fly book, lunch, raincoat, Solunar Tables, fishing calendar, fish finder, can of worms, and one small trout.

- It is true that a guide is a conservationist in disguise.

- It is not true that he takes you where they were biting well "last week," that he encourages you to return "next week" when the water will be "lower," "higher," "clearer," "muddier."

- It is not true that boots are what you wear to carry large quantities of water and are guaranteed to keep your feet warmer in summer and colder in winter.

- It is not true that flies are feather or bucktail imitations of nothing ever seen before.

- It is true that they are the favorite food of moths and are tied especially for decorating fishermen's hats.

- It is true that plugs are imitations of bees, beetles, birds, bananas, cigars, and hula dancers.

- It is true that "rod" is the name for a fishing pole costing over five dollars. It is said, too, that fly rods are sold by weight—the lighter the rod, the heavier the price.

- It is true that the worm is greatly scorned in fishing circles but is secretly used by most trout fishermen.

ADVICE FROM AN ANGLER: To avoid having your canoe capsize unexpectedly, lash two fully leafed tree branches to the stern of the craft. These act as a stabilizer and they may be cut away and discarded when no longer needed.

ORIGINS OF FLY CASTING

Sir Izaak Walton is the patron saint of the angler. His great contribution to angling was his famous book *The Compleat Angler,* first published in 1653. Since that date, hundreds of different editions of this work have been published. In his time, there were some good fly casters and excellent fly fishing in England, but since then angling methods both abroad and in the United States have improved so tremendously that today we are faced with the problem of supplying enough fish. There are better-designed fly rods to go with the improved techniques for dry-fly fishing, wet-fly fishing, bass-bug casting, and salt-water fly casting.

Let's compare. Sir Izaak Walton was content to fish in the streams of the British Isles. The late Lee Wulff fished for Atlantic salmon in the waters of Newfoundland, New Brunswick, and Nova Scotia, then went in for giant-tuna fishing in Nova Scotia, and then flew his Cub plane to fish for bonefish on the flats of the Florida Keys. He used the same fly-rod equipment for bonefish that he did for Atlantic salmon, except that in the North he used his own flies, called White Wulff and Gray Wulff, but in Florida he used a fly that looked like a shrimp and was tied by Homer Rhode, famous bonefish guide in Miami.

Wulff compared his two outings as follows: "My reactions were geared to the fight of an Atlantic salmon, generally considered top fish in fresh waters. While I could let a salmon take line out between my fingers without having the braided nylon burn me, the speed of the bonefish was much greater. After burning my fingers on that first bonefish run, I let the click act as a brake and watched my fly line melt off the reel arbor. I'm not going to give up Atlantic salmon fishing, but every winter or spring from now on I'll spend some time in the warm salt shallows after bonefish, with a fly-casting outfit."

OUTFIT

The type of outfit you select for fly fishing is entirely dependent on the kind of fishing you plan to do. Salmon outfits are bigger, can be used for bonefishing, and are good even in the taking of tarpon and sailfish if you are careful. The rod for dry-fly and wet-fly fishing for trout and bass should be 8 or 8½ feet long, with enough stiffness in the body of the rod to give sufficient striking power, but the action of the rod should permit a delicate presentation of the fly.

The fly reel may be simple, single action with a permanent click, with weight enough to balance the rod properly and capacity enough to hold the fly line. The average rule is: the weight of the reel, line, and filler and the fly should be about 1½ times the weight of the rod. There are several semi-automatics that give you fingertip control.

The fly line is important in casting. In bait casting, you depend on the weight of the lure to get distance, but in fly casting, the weight of the line takes out the fly. Here again, we have it all over Sir Izaak Walton, because we have learned a lot about line finishes, line materials, and line tapers. It is possible for the beginner today to step up and cast a fly that goes out like a bullet. Level lines (the diameter is uniform throughout its length) are for fly fishing with spinners. Tapered lines are for longer casts.

THE BEST TIME TO GO FLY FISHING

Conditions such as muddy waters from heavy rains, a falling barometer, the moon in the wrong phase, and water temperatures that are too warm are exceptions, but generally speaking, the best time to go fishing is whenever you can get away when the season is open, when there is a run on, or when the stream is having a hatch of insects. The best hour for brook-trout fishing is in the evening, as well as for about three hours after sunrise. For rainbows, the evening again, but also all through the day, is generally good. Brown trout bite best at night and are good feeders in early evening. Cutthroats and Dolly Vardens, it seems, are always hungry.

CAST UPSTREAM OR DOWN?

In casting, try to drop your fly in the placid waters of pools or overhanging embankments near swift-running water. Often, you can get a strike in quiet waters when the fish won't bite in the rapids.

In general, the quiet waters require you to fish upstream and fast waters make it necessary to fish downstream, but there is more to it, of course. In the East, where streams are more heavily fished, you will find anglers fishing upstream; the same is true in Wisconsin—or wherever the fish are shy. In the western streams, there are more fish and you can fish up or down, depending on the speed of the current. Edward R. Hewitt, the old master and inventor of the spider fly, used to find a real slick piece of water before tossing his famous spider—upstream. If there is a trout nearby, there is an explosion and the trout is hooked.

FLIES AND HOOKS

In our country, the best way to find out the best flies is to ask an angler who has previously fished the waters. Every angler has a pet list of his own. Our most popular fly patterns today are: Royal Coachman, Ginger Quill, Brown Hackle, Parmachene Belle, McGinty, Queen of the Waters, Black Gnat, Gray Hackle, Coachman, and Professor.

Most fly fishermen on dark days select darker-colored flies, because really all the fish sees is the silhouette, and the surface

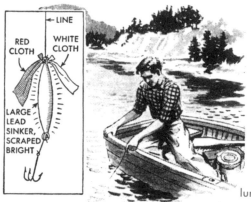

Walleyes lie in wait for minnows near the bottom of the water, and chugging with a combination of natural and artificial bait usually results in a good catch. To assemble a chugging lure, first take a heavy sinker—one large enough to carry the line to the bottom—and scrape it bright. After tying the sinker to the end of the line, attach two small strips of cloth at the upper end of the sinker, one white and the other red. Then fasten a single or treble hook to the lower ring of the sinker. The hook is baited with a minnow, frog, worms, or pork rings. To chug, allow the boat to drift while raising and lowering the bait slowly so that it touches the bottom about every two feet. Varying the movements, slow to fast, often gives good results.

of the water takes on a silvery color, so bright flies will not be seen as well. Black Gnats, Black Hackle, and Black Prince are popular. Bright flies on bright days are always good for rainbows. When going for steelheads, select flies that sink swiftly, preferably flies that have lead- or copper-wrapped bodies, because these fish are usually well beneath the surface. Spinners are often used, but these drag along the bottom and you can easily get hung on a rock, whereas a weighted fly bumps along more on the bottom.

Hook sizes that get the most fish are 10 to 16, but when fishing in steams above five thousand feet you must use smaller

HOW TO CAST

These five "clock' sketches show how to cast with a fly rod. Above, at the beginning of the cast, lift the rod slightly to 10 o'clock to gain tension for pickup.

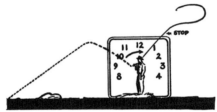

During the pickup, snap the rod tip sharply upward from 10 to 1 o'clock, using a brisk upswing of the forearm without moving the upper arm or shoulder.

After this back cast, pause for a moment while the line continues to move and whips out behind you. This will clear the line and prepare it for the forward cast.

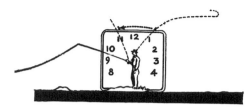

To cast the line forward again, drive the rod tip forward but not downward, stopping at 9:30 o'clock. Apply power to your cast between 1 and 11 o'clock.

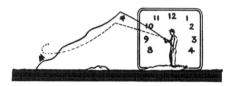

In laying the fly, aim three feet above the water target. As the line is about to reach the limit of the cast, raise the rod tip slightly so that the fly hits the water first.

flies, usually from 14 to 20, because the natural hatches above this sea-level measurement—drakes and stone flies—are tiny. In the streams of California, Montana, Wyoming, and Idaho, the anglers prefer sizes 16 to 18. Anglers who want trout generally match the size of bugs hatching or nymphs being eaten.

Early-season anglers are the ones who must be most particular that their dry fly imitates the natural insect. The hatches are most numerous in May and June. Later in the year, when the fish are feeding on grasshoppers and other bugs, the trout are not so fussy about what they take.

In 1936, John Alden Knight came forth with his much-respected theory that fish feed during certain periods. These time charts—now widely published—are called the Solunar Tables, and they tell you when during the day you should fish.

No one has yet developed a successful fish call like a duck call or a moose call, but Frank Steel had an instrument called the "Fish Finder" that makes fishing sound easy. For a time, he held the world record for chinook salmon, with an 83-pounder that he caught in 1910 in the Umpqua River. He was the former national fly-casting champion, and he backed the instrument with many years of experience in fishing.

He said, "You've got to find the fish before you can catch them, so I have developed a dependable way of locating bass, trout, walleyes, northern pike, muskies, and panfish. I found the favorite water temperatures of all the common freshwater game fish. All smallmouth bass like 67 degrees, and they like it the same across the continent. When the surface water is 60 degrees, you will find the smallmouth bass

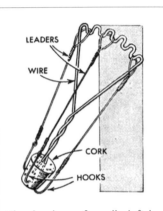

The leaders of snelled fishhooks will not become tangled when carried in a tackle box if they are kept in a holder like this one. It consists of a length of wire shaped as indicated in a cork.

five to ten feet deep, so you must fish for them at that depth. The Fish Finder gives you a water thermometer and the necessary fish charts for each fish."

What looks most important to the fish is the fly. It takes a good fly, properly presented, to get the best out of fly fishing. Fly tying is not just a fad of fishermen; it's a hobby that has lured doctors, presidents, baseball players, lawyers, and industrialists away from their work. Every American town in a trout-fishing area possesses a fly tier or two, and the big cities are crowded with them. In fact, the bug that bites the fly tier produces a fever every bit as serious as the disease that strikes millions of fishermen as soon as the season opens.

The basic methods used in fly tying are simple, and the tools are few. The materials at first can be those you find easily at hand—a few feathers from a hunting neighbor's mallard duck, along with some bits of thread and floss from your wife's sewing basket. As with every hobby, the equipment and materials can become increasingly elaborate and expensive—some fly tiers wind up deigning to use only a particular tail feather from a particular kind of peacock. At first, you'll copy standard makes of flies, but sooner or later you'll be dreaming up your own.

For a start, you'll need a fly-tying vise. A pair of small, needle-nose pliers, a picking tool made of a needle pushed into a lollipop-stick handle, a safety-razor blade, and two pairs of scissors—one small straight-bladed pair and one pair of manicure scissors—will meet the rest of your beginning tool needs.

You'll have to make a careful study of the parts of a fly—there are more than you would think could be ascribed to a hook decked with fur and feathers. You'll have to learn the place and purpose of the tag, butt, tail, joint, hackle, body, ribbing, wing, cheek, topping, horns, head, and eye.

Some of the materials used for fly bodies included

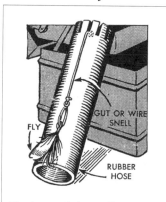

To keep fishing flies from becoming entangled, use a simple holder made from a piece of garden hose. Slip the hooks over one end of the hose, and notch the other end to take the knotted end of the gut.

tinsel, silk floss, fur, chenille, wool, quill, and cork. As the name indicates, fly hackles are almost always made from the hackle feathers of various kinds of fowl. Tails, on the other hand, are composed of feathers from necks, breasts, and wings, as well as the tails of birds. These are trimmed and fitted and tied down with fly-tying silk, then covered with a good grade of fly-tying wax. You have your choice of several hundred different fly patterns, plus those you can create yourself.

Carry small fishhooks in an empty matchbook. Stick a small wad of beeswax inside the matchbook, insert the barbed ends of the hooks in the wax, and close the cover.

Flies are delicate tackle and need care. Protect them from moths, which will quickly strip all the feathers and other materials down to the bare hook unless they are stored with plenty of moth repellent. To restore flies that have become matted or crushed, hold them over live steam. This will restore their luster and shape. After fishing, dry flies between blotting paper.

Chapter 11

BAIT CASTING

It was the place and time a bass fisherman finds only in his dreams. Only this wasn't a dream. It was the real thing. It was the glory of a summer sunset coloring the water, the dimple of feeding bass, the little rings spreading over the golden red surface of the bay.

It was the roll of dorsal fins, the lusty slap of a forked tail, the sudden leap of a heavy fish at a minnow skipping across the surface of the water.

Now was the time to snap on a small wiggly plug and cast it into those rings. It was bass feeding time.

Not so many years ago, bait casting was just another way to catch muskellunge, northern pike, pickerel, walleyes, lake trout, white bass, panfish, largemouth bass, smallmouth bass, and spotted bass, but in recent years our fishermen have made it the most popular form of fishing. Now, with a bait-casting outfit, you can catch dozens of the saltwater game fish, including tarpon, snook, bonefish, ladyfish, barracuda, weakfish, snappers, and others, if you fish in Florida.

It is an easy sport to learn, and millions of fishermen are luring the fish with plugs, spoons, spinners, feathers, bucktails, rubber worms, and pork strips. Usually, one quick lesson will do it—then practice makes for perfection. You must remember to keep a slight thumb pressure on the spool of the reel to prevent a backlash (overspin), often referred to as a "bird's nest." Bait casting is easy to master; however, just in case you happen to be the impatient type and you fail to become an expert after three casts, the manufacturers now have an answer—level-wind reels that won't backlash.

It is not only the art of bait casting that attracts the lads and lasses to this popular sport, but also the environment. It offers a panorama of beauty from the glacial lakes of Alaska to the mountain lakes in the Rockies, the ten thousand jewels and gems of Minnesota, and the colorful flats of Florida.

If you want action in fishing, none of that sitting all day soaking live bait—give bait casting your best efforts. If you want action from a fish that leaps, rears, flips, and bucks, try your luck at bass fishing. Any kind of bass fishing will do, whether it be for white bass, spotted bass, largemouth bass, or smallmouth bass. If you have a bait-casting rod that you prize highly, don't use it when going after big bass, because sometimes the smallmouth (bronzeback) or even the largemouth (lunker) just ain't no gentleman. If you have never been in the ring with a black bass, put on your fishing togs, go to a lake where there are bass, and climb into your corner. If you tie into one, you will find him a real battler.

ADVICE FROM AN ANGLER: As fish under a certain size are not allowed to be taken from most lakes and streams, a scale painted on your fishing rod to measure those of doubtful length may save you some embarrassment if an officer questions the size of some of the fish in your catch. Starting near the reel, lay off the scale on a white background, marking the figures and division lines in black.

HISTORY OF BAIT CASTING

Let's run over the history of fishing to see how bait casting fits in. The hooks that we often see in museums, made from the bones of animals and the beaks of birds, are proof enough that fishing first began in prehistoric times. We have also seen picture stories of fishing dating back to the days of the Egyptians, about 3000 B.C., and these pictures on rocks show fishing rods and lines as well as fish. The first book on fishing to be printed in English was *A Treatyse of Fysshynge Wyth an Angle,* by Dame Juliana Berners—in 1496.

The first fishing rod of split bamboo was made in the United States by Samuel Phillippi of Easton, Pennsylvania, in 1848. The first split-bamboo bass rod was made by Charles F. Murphy of Newark, New Jersey, in 1866 and consisted of four glued strips of bamboo. Hiram Leonard of Bangor, Maine, made the first six-strip bamboo rod. Dr. James Alexander Henshall, the father of black-bass fishing in this country, made the first six-strip bait-casting rod in 1875. It was about seven feet long. Charles F. Orvis made the first of these that sold in the stores.

Although split-bamboo bait-casting rods are still considered among the best for this purpose, the most popular casting rods today are made of graphite, because most of them are stronger and they duplicate the sporty action of split bamboo. They also cost less.

The first reel ever made was carved out of a block of wood and had a handle for turning the block. The first multiplying reel used for bait casting was made by George Snyder in 1810. He was a watchmaker living in Paris, Kentucky, and his reel was so geared that the spool revolved four times for every turn of the handle. Jonathan Meek, B. F. Meek, and W. H. Talbot came along with multiplying reels that are still in use here and there by old-timers who enjoy the ever-increasing sport of tournament casting.

The no-backlash feature on many of the reels made today has proved to be of great help to the millions of fishermen who enjoy casting a spoon or a plug into the lily pads for their small-mouth bass. This reel makes a novice look like a professional in ten minutes. I have a personal preference for the smaller-size reels with the level-wind feature for muskie fishing. Before you go fishing, oil your reel. Keep it in a cloth bag and then drop it in a leather container. It will last longer.

Fishing lines for bait casting were once made of twisted horsehair and braided silk, cotton, and linen. Then braided fishing lines made their entrance, braided of silk and nylon, and treated in a way that makes them more water resistant than ever before. Today, monofilament and fluorocarbon are the lines of choice.

The first plug was called the "200" and was carved out of wood by Jim Heddon of Dowagiac, Michigan. Why he named it that, no one seems to know. Later, he carved a bait similar in appearance, put spinners on it, and called it the Dowagiac. This was the first underwater bait ever put on the market. Today, there are hundreds of bait makers who have imitated everything that swims, and then some. There are designs resembling a swimming frog, mouse, chipmunk, duck, sucker, crab, minnow, crippled minnow, and many others. The first plugs were made of white cedar, but today most of them are plastic. Never before have anglers and fish had such a choice of lures.

Catching a largemouth bass requires a rather slow retrieve

ADVICE FROM AN ANGLER: The nature of some fish to investigate a shiny object can be utilized by the still-fisherman to attract them to his baited hook. A good way to do this is to crimp a bright bottle cap over the lead sinker. Be sure the edges of the cap do not touch the line and wear it in two.

HOW TO BAIT CAST

The overhead cast is the most important one, and it should be mastered first. The panel at left, from top to bottom, shows the proper arm and rod movement to execute a good cast. At the beginning, the arm should be close to the side, with the forearm parallel with the ground. Then bring the rod up briskly, with the wrist acting as a hinge. The movement is straight over the right shoulder. Stop the rod when the handle is straight up, and immediately begin the forward cast, starting slowly but increasing the speed. Apply the thumb lightly to the spool while the lure is in flight, to prevent a backlash. Keep your eyes constantly on the target, and hold the rod in alignment with the outgoing line. A good average cast travels about seventy-five feet.

off the lure; a little faster retrieve for smallmouth bass; and a much faster one for white bass, walleyes, pickerel, northern pike, and muskies. A bait caster gets his full reward on earth when a big game fish hits his surface lure. There is an explosion on the surface of the water, and the fight is on.

Make sure your tackle box has a few weedless plugs and spoons for fishing in lily pads and weeds. And be certain your box has some lures of all sizes, from those for panfish up to the muskie and tarpon size.

To be properly equipped, a bait caster should have two complete outfits—one for casting lures that weigh from a half ounce up to an ounce, and the second for casting heavier lures for muskies, northern pike, tarpon, barracuda, and snook. The trend today is toward smaller lures that require less effort to cast. The exception to this trend is found in Florida, where the bass in fresh water run up to 16 and 18 pounds and the saltwater fish now and then tip the scales at close to 100 pounds. The expert or the stunt fisherman may use these small lures with light rods and fast reels for big fish, but we recommend having two outfits.

FISH AVAILABLE TO THE BAIT CASTER

You can catch bass, crappies, bluegills, rock bass, perch, pickerel, northern pike, lake trout, and all the saltwater species that come into the bays, bayous, rivers, canals, and ditches, but you really haven't fished until you've taken a muskellunge on light tackle.

My favorite fish is called by a great many different names: muskellunge, maskinonge (Canada), muskie, muskalonge, masqueallonge (French Canadian), lune, kinonge, mascanonge, mascallonge, muskallonge, maskenosha, muscallunge, noscanonge, and dozens more.

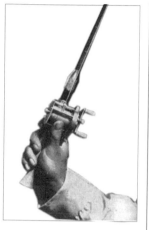

When preparing for a cast, hold the rod with the reel handles up, and carry through the cast with the reel in the same position. This will give the reel its best action, as it will ride smoothly on its bearing. Note that the thumb presses lightly against the spool.

The muskie is a top freshwater game fish—always ready for a fight. Because of its size, running up to 100 pounds, it is the biggest of all freshwater game fish.

With the possible exception of bonefish addicts or tarpon enthusiasts, no anglers are more enthusiastic about fishing than those who go for muskies. At least a million have caught the great tiger-stripped battler, and now they are afflicted with "muskellunge-itis." There is but one cure. A doctor's prescription for these victims reads: "Three weeks in Ontario in July, August, or September on any of the following streams or lakes: Lake of the Woods, Lake Manitou, Eagle Lake, the Vermilion lakes, Lac Seul, Cliff Lake, Georgian Bay, French River, or Lake Nipissing."

There is nothing meaner or tougher than a muskie, unless it's the saltwater ruffian of a brother called the greater barracuda. It's the fightin'est of fish that ever tore a plug to pieces. It's no wonder muskies are so often called "tackle busters."

Muskie tackle is special. A 5- or 5½-foot rod with a stiff backbone is best. A level-wind, quadruple-multiplying reel is just right. A 12-inch wire leader is essential. A 15- or 18-pound-test line is good for a 60-pound fish. Use large plugs or spoons: surface plugs, sub-surface plugs, and deep-running plugs, spoons, or bucktails. Muskie plugs and spoons should weigh at least an ounce, and they can be an ounce and a half.

All in all, the muskellunge provides quite a challenge to the game fisherman. To the great strength and agility of this fish is added its ability to twist and fight and dodge in relatively shallow waters. In addition to the likelihood of the muskie pulling itself free, there is plenty of added chance that it will be aided by snags and obstructions in the weeds and underbrush of shallow water. The muskie fisherman's best strategy, therefore, is to run the fish away and head it into deeper water. It is easy to see from this why muskie fishing requires special line and tackle.

When a muskie strikes, anything can happen. The big tail lashes the water to a foam. The meanest sight of all is a muskie that takes off and heads for the boat. Until you know its intentions, it's just a question of what to do—when and if. Many an angler has tossed his whole outfit in the water and wanted no more of muskie fishing. And many a muskie has driven straight for the boat and then leaped out of the water so high that it clears the craft. Others have landed inside.

When one wild muskie landed in a rowboat, the excited fisherman whipped out his six-shooter and let Mr. Muskie have it; then he and the guide had to row for shore to save themselves from drowning.

Muskies are a favorite sport and food fish and are found in weed beds and on bars in lakes and rivers of the north country.

The northern muskellunge (*Esox immaculatus*) has a golden bronze appearance, often with reddish fins and tail, and inhabits the waters of Wisconsin and Minnesota, as well as from the Mississippi basin northward almost to Hudson Bay.

The Chautauqua or Ohio muskie (*Esox ohiensis*) is yellowish green in color and has a barred pattern that resembles worm tracks. It is found in the waters of the Ohio River and in many of its tributaries in New York, Ohio, Pennsylvania, Indiana, West Virginia, Kentucky, Alabama, Tennessee, and North Carolina.

The St. Lawrence muskie (*Esox masquinongy*) is silvery and gray-green in color and is found in the upper St. Lawrence River, parts of the Great Lakes, and some of the rivers and lakes of eastern Ontario and western Quebec. It is famous in Lake Nipissing, Lake Ontario, the Niagara River, and French River.

The new muskie, the True Tiger (*Esox masquinongy amentus*), discovered by Mike Ament of Sioux Lookout, Ontario, is a subspecies of the northern muskie. I have caught a dozen of them myself and can attest to the vast differences. There are two different muskies in Muskie Lake and in Little Lake Vermilion—the northern muskie and the True Tiger. The latter has a white skin with tigerlike bars that stand out like the stripes of a zebra. The body is shorter and the fish is heavy. The head is large for the length of the fish, and the fighting qualities are greater. Biologists who have studied the differences agree—we have found a new muskie.

Nail an old rubber heel onto the stern of your rowboat and use it to squeeze water out of your fishline after each trip. The heel is slit, as shown in the circular detail.

Chapter 12

SPIN CASTING

They call it spin fishing, and experts who have been watching sportsmen rise to the bait predicted that Americans would become a nation of spin fishermen, bar a few diehards who refuse to try anything new. And just that has come to pass.

What has made spin fishing (or just plain spinning) dart ahead in popularity during the past years?

It completely lacks the backlash bogey—you just can't backlash or overrun a spinning reel. It enables a fly fisherman to stand on the bank and flip a weighted trout fly far out into a mountain stream. It allows the surf caster to reach out beyond the heavy surf. It lets the sportsman use the lightest possible tackle in taking the largest possible fish. And any man, using just one rod and reel, can bait-cast, fly-fish, surf-cast, troll, mooch, drift, or still-fish, using any kind of lure from wet or dry flies to plugs, spoons, spinners, and live or cut baits.

The fun of spin fishing is the lightness of the line against the pull of a big fish, and the heart of spin fishing is the reel. Essentially, all fishing reels are spools, similar to a spool of thread. Ordinarily, when you pull thread off a spool, the spool itself revolves. This is the principle of a conventional bait-casting reel. But if you hold a spool at one end and pull the thread directly off the other, the thread spirals out quickly and easily with the spool remaining stationary. This is the principle of a spin-fishing reel.

Because friction is virtually eliminated in a spinning reel, the angler can make extremely long casts with miniature lures. They can be weighted flies, streamers, small plugs or spoons, and a great variety of new spinning, wobbling, limping, and popping lures that are imported from France, Switzerland, Great Britain, Belgium, Sweden, and Germany. By attaching a plastic float to the line near his lure, the spin fisherman can float his fly long distances from shore or boat and cover water that would be impossible to reach with a fly rod.

In spin fishing, the lightest lines from a 2- to 10-pound test are used without much fear of breakage, even by large fish, because the reel gives off line as fast as the fish jerks or pulls. It's no surprise today to hear of an extremely large white marlin being taken on a 10-pound-test monofilament line, or three-foot rainbows and 40-pound chinook salmon brought in on 6-pound-test braided nylon.

GARDEN HOSE

ROPE

Several sections of discarded garden hose strung on a length of clothesline provide a portable seat, which is just the thing when fishing from the bank of a river or lake. Cut hose sections to size and drill two holes through each of them. Then string clothesline through the holes and knot the ends to form a handle for the seat.

The fishermen of North America are participating in the establishment of a new major outdoor sport. Many millions of just plain folks have gone in for spin fishing. There are at least fifty spinning reels now made in this country, Canada, Australia, Britain, France, Italy, Switzerland, Belgium, Sweden, Germany, and Japan. Spin-fishing rods, from six to nine feet long, are made of hollow glass, bamboo, solid glass, and tubular steel. Most of them have extremely large guides to decrease friction as the line whispers out. The lines themselves are mostly nylon monofilament, braided nylon, and imported platyl monofilament.

Although fishermen in most parts of this country are just waking up to spin fishing, it isn't exactly a new sport. The English and French started spin fishing about 1905. There was an early French model of a spinning reel, but the most famous of the early fixed-spool reels was the Illingsworth, which was made in Britain.

In 1933, I had the pleasure of casting a Hardy Altex, an English reel, and at that time there were few sportsmen in America who had even heard of spin fishing. The reel was amazingly easy to use. A quick flip of the wrist sent out a beautiful and sparkling little invitation to a fish 120 feet across the bay.

In spinning, the line is wound around a fixed spool. The axis on the spool is parallel to the rod. When the handle of the open-face reel is turned after a cast, a mechanical finger (pickup bail) automatically picks up the line to rewind it on the spool. To prepare for the next cast, the bail is merely pushed out of the way so the line can spiral off the spool freely.

When a fish strikes, an automatic and adjustable clutch permits it to run line off the reel. Thus, if the angler is reeling in a fish and it decides to make a long run, the line spirals off under tension, despite the fact that the angler may still be retrieving. Thus, for the first time in fishing, there's a real balance between the fish and the tackle.

The theory of spin fishing hasn't changed much since the early days, but the rods and reels, lines and lures, are being made of new materials. One of the latest reels is made exclusively of nylon and glass fiber, weighs only 4 ounces, operates smoothly, requires no lubrication for the life of the reel, and is impervious to salt water. There's nothing in it to rust or corrode.

The best spinning rods are similar in action to a good rod designed for dry-fly fishing, but with more power in the mid-section and the butt, as well as plenty of action in the tip. It's a rod that is between a bait-casting rod and a fly rod in length, being stiffer than a fly rod and much lighter in action than most bait-casting rods. Don't buy a rod with small guides for an open-face spinning reel. Big guides are essential, because the line whirls off the spool at a terrific speed and small guides can't pass it that fast.

In selecting a spin-fishing reel, choose the one that suits your own type of fishing. Don't send a boy to do a man's job; buy a larger reel if you plan to do heavy saltwater fishing. It's possible, though, to do some saltwater fishing with freshwater spinning tackle, now so popular in all the protected waters off Florida. If you do so, remember to get a reel that is saltwater proof or at minimum rinse it thoroughly in freshwater after every day's fishing.

Most of the imported reels are open-face; that is, the spool has no cover. Some of the popular American- and Canadian-made reels are covered, three of them with a cone-shaped casing.

Right- and left-hand reels are somewhat confusing. A right-handed person normally will buy a right-hand reel which, oddly enough, is so constructed that he or she turns the handle with the left hand. This is so the fish can be played with the stronger right hand on the rod while reeling in with the left. Sometimes a die-hard bait caster will deliberately buy a left-hand reel, merely because he can't overcome the habit of reeling with the

HOW TO SPIN CAST

Learn the overhand cast first. The lure should be about a foot from the tip of the rod. Now hold the rod in your right hand (assuming you are right-handed), with the reel hanging under the handle of the rod. Two fingers should be on each side of the stem that supports the reel. Next, press the line against the rod with your forefinger and disengage the bail pickup. This leaves the line free to spin off the reel, as soon as you release it by straightening your finger as you finish the forward cast.

Bring the rod straight up to the 12 o'clock position with a sweeping, but quick, motion, then flick the wrist forward until the rod is at a 45-degree angle. Point your finger at the target, which releases the line and permits the lure to shoot out. You'll be amazed at the distance you get with your first cast. The lure can be slowed down or stopped on ▶ the target by touching your forefinger to the reel spool.

Your rod and hand should be in this position just after the lure is released. Before starting to reel in, raise the tip of the rod while holding the line with your forefinger to straighten the line. Now, start reeling in the line. To avoid twisted line, do not "crank" your fish in, but "pump" it in with the rod tip, reeling in the slack line.

right hand. One reel, the Ambidex, is so constructed that the handle can be installed on either side. And many reels are available with either a left- or right-hand crank to suit the angler.

OUTFIT

It's far easier to master a spinning outfit than a bait-casting outfit, because there's no chance of backlash. When you're ready for your initial cast with an open-face reel, first check the drag adjustment. It should be set under the test strength of the line, so that if you get an unexpected strike, your line won't snap. On the other hand, the drag should be firm enough to hook a fish.

When the bait has reached the water, reel in the slack line and drop the rod tip to a horizontal position, preparatory to hooking a fish. If you get a strike, jerk the rod very gently. Most fish will run off the line, and the drag of the reel will slow them down. Don't crank the handle while the fish is taking out line—wait until it tires, or you'll put extra twists in your line.

A side cast will give you good distance if you have proper timing. In this cast, swing your rod tip out and up like a plane taking off, and when your rod tip has reached its maximum speed, release the line. Raise the rod tip as the lure hits the water.

The underhand cast is used when shrubbery or trees prevent a conventional cast. Lower the tip of the rod and allow the lure to hang two feet from the rod tip. Start swinging the lure back and forth, then flip it out with a quick wrist motion.

In the lariat cast, the lure is twirled at the end of the rod until you can flip it. At that moment, the rod tip must be pointed straight out.

If you really want to pop the eyes of your bait-casting friends, try the bow-and-arrow cast. Hold the lure carefully by the bend of the hook or hooks and pull it back beside the reel so the rod is flexed. Release it suddenly, and the lure will shoot far out across the water, powered by the snap of the rod.

There are a few basic differences in casting the closed-face reel. This type of reel eliminates line flapping and loss of line on a windy day. It can also be fitted to a fly rod, as the line pays out from one point and big guides aren't necessary. This permits the angler to pack a fly rod, a fly reel, and a spinning reel for fishing variety on the same trip.

The non-reverse on some closed reels is operated by a knurled ring located between the crank and the cover plate. You adjust the drag on this type of reel by stripping off line with the crank in reverse. A clicking sound means the pickup is revolving, although the crank is stationary. Set the drag just tight enough to retrieve your lure. Just before you cast, release the non-reversing crank. To find the casting position, turn the crank forward to the 3 o'clock position. You will hear a clicking as you overpower the drag. Now reverse the direction until the crank snaps into the casting position at about 5 o'clock, and make your cast as with an open-face reel.

LINE TWIST

Most spin fishermen will recognize only one drawback to spinning, but it's important that you know about line twist and how to overcome it. Each time the pickup revolves around the reel, it puts a twist in the line, but this straightens out when you cast. A great many lures, such as devons and spinners, will twist the line as they move through the water. Eventually, the line may twist to such a point that it may shrivel into tight loops. Then there are those times when the fish is running out of line and you carelessly reel in. More twist.

To overcome line twist, it is better to wind new line on a spool by hand or with a lathe than with the reel itself. There are many good spin fishermen who don't completely agree with this; they put line on a reel by twisting it on with the pickup, figuring they can straighten the line when they cast out.

Many of the spinning lures are loaded so that the weight is off center, to combat line twist. Some are made in pairs: twin lures that look exactly alike, yet one revolves to the left and the other to the right. You fish with one for a while, then switch to the other and work the twist out of the line. Other lures have keels, which keep them from revolving but permit a blade to spin. Bead-chain swivels are very effective in preventing line twist and even more effective when used with keel-type lures. Some use the ball-bearing swivels. When you complete a retrieve, keep the rod tip as high as possible to untwist the line.

After each hour of spin fishing, you'll be wise if you remove the lure and let out the line in a current or trail it over the stern of a moving boat until all the line twist comes out. Most fishermen carry extra spools of line for changing during a day of fishing, especially if they are going after fish of different sizes, in which case they change the weight of the line to fit the circumstance.

THE LASTEST RAGE

Spin fishing has really taken hold on the Pacific Coast. Don Harger, a widely known fishing authority in Salem, Oregon, says that spinning on the West Coast has grown from the novelty stage to a point where it now leads all other angling methods by a wide margin. Down Florida way, Homer Rhode, an all-around angler in Miami, reports that fishermen in the southeastern part of the nation have gone overboard for spinning, and they are taking pompano from the bridges, bonefish and permit on the Keys flats, snook along the canals, tarpon up the rivers, and sailfish, white marlin, wahoo, and dolphin in the Gulf Stream, all on monofilament line of less than 12-pound test.

Ted Williams, the former Boston slugger, who also specialized in catching anything that swims, once told me, "It's even more fun than fishing with my fly rod." Joe Bates Jr. of Longmeadow,

If you use a bamboo fishing pole, the hollow butt end is a safe place in which to carry extra fishhooks. The pole is cut off just above one of the joints, leaving a hollow section to the next joint. Hooks of average sizes can be placed in this hollow portion, where they are held by stopping the opening with a cork of suitable size.

CORK

BAMBOO POLE

Massachusetts, one of America's leading authorities on spin fishing, says, "Any fisherman not equipped with spinning gear is a bit old-fashioned." Clare Bryan of Chicago, who caught a 34-pound, 10-ounce white marlin on an 11-pound-test monofilament line, says, "Soon spin fishermen will be catching 100-pound saltwater fish on 11-pound-test line." Ross D. Siragusa, whose art and skill at big-game fishing for tuna won him the distinction of top honors in the Cat Cay Tuna Tournament, says, "Using 6-pound-test monofilament and a 4-ounce split-bamboo spinning rod makes bonefishing look easy." And M. Ray Applegate of Muncie, Indiana, who spins for bonefish at Bimini, Walker Cay, Florida Keys, and in Hawaii, says, "Sixteen bonefish in one day is easy with a spin-fishing outfit but would be difficult with any other tackle. It's lucky for fishing that spin fishermen return their catch to the water."

Spinning can't guarantee that you'll take more fish or bigger ones; fortunately, the lure of fishing has always been that the angler is pitting his wits and ability against an untamed opponent. But spinning will guarantee one thing—you'll have a lot more fun playing this age-old game of fishing.

Chapter 13

SALTWATER FISHING

Life is too short not to find time for saltwater fishing. There is a mystery about the sea that forever lures the angler. The all-connecting waters of the oceans, seas, bays, and coves may lead to a sudden and surprising catch. Starting out to fish for snook, the angler may end up with a record tarpon; searching for a mackerel, he may boat a broadbill swordfish, rarest of all the sea's great angling trophies.

The big, swift, ocean-roving fish may be caught in sheltered inland waters, where they occasionally congregate, but they are normally sought in their natural feeding haunts in the open sea. The catch may be measured in pounds or hundreds of pounds, but the pleasure of the sport can never be measured in numbers—only in its thrills.

The bonefish has long been near the top of the list of the ocean's sporting fish. It is blessed with a speed that few can equal. It is shy and difficult to approach, and it is caught in warm, shallow, quiet waters where fishing conditions are close to ideal. For many years, bonefish have been caught on special rods and light, matching lines coupled with reels that cast the lightly weighted baits near the fish without alarming them. In recent seasons, standard freshwater fly-fishing tackle has been used to hook and hold them. Since they are far swifter than any freshwater fish is known to be, this opens up a new field to ambitious anglers.

Homer Rhode Jr. of Coral Gables, Florida, pioneered this type of fishing and developed a special streamer-type fly that closely imitates in shape and action the shrimp on which the bonefish feed. Nowadays, there are many successful bonefish flies, such as Clouser Minnows, Gotchas, and Cray Charlies.

The most successful plugs in bonefishing are the zaragossa type (surface plugs). These plugs are so balanced that they can be worked equally well on or beneath the surface. The best retrieve is over grass beds and small channels on the flats, with a moderate zigzag surface retrieve for a distance of about thirty or forty feet, then smashing the plug underneath, working it in an erratic manner, and increasing the tempo of the retrieve to an extremely rapid pace.

For casting the channels from midstream to the banks, a red-headed yellow feather is best. This is the same type that is used in Florida waters for pompano and bluefish. Big bonefish are seen regularly in the waters of the Florida Keys.

Bonefish tackle (a 4-ounce casting rod and 6-thread line, or a bass-weight fly rod with two hundred yards or more of backing and 15-pound-test leader next to the fly) will also give an angler all the thrills he needs if he hooks into any of the other game fish in the same waters, such as the ladyfish, permit, barracuda, snook, or tarpon.

Tarpon are among the ocean's best performers. They strike artificial baits, can be caught by light casting tackle, and are swift in their runs and endlessly spectacular in their leaps. Because their mouths are hard and bony, they are both hard to hook and hard to hold. All these sporting qualities are combined in a silvery fish that goes up to a record weight of 286 pounds, taken in Rubane, Guinea-Bissau, Africa, on March 20, 2003. The tarpon

Have you ever had trouble losing your bait can in the grass or weeds while still-fishing along the banks of a stream? If so, just cut a stake from a tree branch, sharpen one end, and attach the can to this with string or a couple of rubber bands. When forced into the bank, the stake will keep the can elevated so that it can be seen from a considerable distance. A piece of white cloth tied to the top of the stake will make it even easier to spot the device.

RUBBER BANDS

frequents the quiet inland or inshore waters, where the great leaps and runs bred of the open sea are accentuated.

Flies and fly rods will take tarpon in the shallow bays and canals or any of the confined waters. Bait-casting rods will cover the same waters, and either rod can be used for tarpon under 50 pounds with regularity; however, when these silvery fish pass the 100-pound mark, either the angler's skill must increase prodigiously or the weight of his tackle must rise to match a heavier foe.

Tarpon in channels and small rivers go for streamer flies on fly rods and for plugs on bait-casting equipment. In the Gulf of Mexico, they hit big plugs and spoons that are trolled. At hot spots such as Boca Grande Pass, it's a game of drifting with live crabs as bait.

There are millions of tarpon along the west coast of Florida in April, May, and June, then along the coasts of Mississippi,

Alabama, and Louisiana in May, June, and July, off Texas from May to September, and off Mexico from March to July.

It was in 1915 that Captain Bill Hatch worked out the drop-back method of fishing and opened the angling door to the sailfish and the marlin. These spearfish tap a bait with their spears and, having stunned it, turn and take it into their mouths. Hatch's development brought the marlin and sailfish, which had previously been considered only nuisances, into the forefront of the big-game-fishing field. Their amazing power to leap thrilled the angling world.

Hatch's discovery changed the contours of the fishing cruisers. They sprouted long, thin bamboo poles that swept out from their decks. The angler's line passes from the rod tip out to the outrigger's tip, where it is held gently by a clothespin. From there it drifts astern to take the bait out to one side of the propeller wash, to hold it high and make it skill like a frightened fish.

When a sailfish or marlin surges up and strikes the bait with his bill, the strike is sharp enough to pull the line free from the clothespin. The slack lets the bait drift in the water while the sailfish turns to take it into his mouth, before the line tightens again. The pressure is timed to come just when the bait is taken.

The sailfish, long and slender, can skitter across the surface of the sea like a skipping stone. The word "tailwalking" was added to our language to describe this sailfish stunt.

There are many varieties of sailfish, but the two most important are Atlantic sailfish and Pacific sailfish. Most Atlantic sails are caught in the blue Gulf Stream waters from Stuart to Key West, Florida, but every summer some of them are caught off the Texas Gulf coast. The pacific sails are most plentiful at Acapulco and Guaymas, Mexico.

The marlin lacks a sailfish's high distinctive dorsal but has it trimmed for strength and speed. Most sailfish fall well below the 100-pound mark; most marlin go well above it—and some go to more than 1,000 pounds. They are heavier throughout and more difficult to handle on the rod and reel.

Striped marlin are found in the warm waters of the world. The biggest ever taken on hook and line weighed 692 pounds—caught off Balboa, California. Blue marlin are found mostly in the Atlantic, between Cuba, Cat Cay, and Florida. The biggest weighed 1,402 pounds—caught off Vitória, Brazil. White marlin are smaller and range from Maryland in the summer to Key West in winter. The biggest weighed 181 pounds and was taken off Vitória, Brazil.

The school tuna, ranging from 10 to more than 100 pounds, suddenly became the public's favorite. They were great sport, they were good food, and there were lots of them to be had. Big tuna are tough. They have a habit of heading for the bottom when exhausted, and only fairly heavy tackle can bring them to the boat. They make no spectacular leaps when hooked; every bit of their abundant energy is turned to racing speed.

Throughout the years, the broadbill swordfish, first caught on fishing tackle in the Catalina area, has remained the greatest trophy of them all. These fish are rare and seldom inclined to strike when found. They are powerful and swift, occasional leapers. Their mouths are soft and difficult to hook. In all the years of fishing in all the waters of the world, less than 350 have been caught by anglers. Like spearfish, the swordfish is caught by using the drop-back method. The average fish is somewhere between 300 and 400 pounds, but the record, from the Humboldt Current near the shores of Chile, weighed 1,182 pounds.

The flounder fisherman, with his simple tackle and his 1-pound catch, shares a thrill with a record holder and his giant fish. The flounder, often called fluke, is one of the best eating fish and therefore is most popular with summer fishermen.

Flounders often hit a trolling feather jig, but mostly they go for a hardhead minnow. The fluke lies in the sand at the bottom, and when a minnow passes by, he streaks after the bait.

One of the most popular ways to fish for flounder is drifting, using a cork that drifts with the tide. Flounders are abundant from Massachusetts to the Carolinas, wherever the inlets have a sandy bottom. They are a light-tackle sport fish, and anglers use a bay rod or a bait-casting rod, a 1/0 reel, and 9-thread line.

Although you can catch fluke while still-fishing with cut bait, by far the most interesting way is with a live bait that is moving. It requires a 2- or 3-ounce sinker and a 1/0 or 2/0 hook. When a fluke strikes, the tugs are sharp, and he has enough flap in his system to come in fighting at the boat.

The weakfish is perhaps the most popular of the small sport fishes along our Atlantic coast. Thousands of anglers catch weakfish in New York, in Peconic Bay, in Gardiner Bay, off the New Jersey coast, in Delaware Bay, and as far south as Cape Hatteras, North Carolina.

The spotted weakfish is most plentiful from Virginia south to Florida, especially off Sea Island, Georgia, Jacksonville Beach, in the Indian River, and off Melbourne.

Light tackle is also used in catching weakfish. Shrimp is the best bait on a very small hook, or you can use a small block tin squid with a worm on the hook. Small fishing plugs are used in Florida.

The top fish of them all, in the opinion of New Englanders and some anglers on the Pacific coast too, is the striped bass. It attracts the special attention of close to a million sportsmen. The range is Maine to the Carolinas, and stripers were introduced in California and are plentiful there.

OUTFIT

You catch stripers surf casting, trolling, and plug casting. For fly casting, you will need a nine-foot, 8- or 9-weight rod, an intermediate sinking line, and a reel with a disc drag and at least

HOW TO CAST

The sketches show the motions off the body during a surf cast. The line should be wet before it is cast. The speed of the right arm is increased until the greatest power is applied as the rod passes perpendicular. At this point, most of the thumb pressure on the reel spool is released.

In surf casting, hold your right hand directly under the reel, with your thumb resting on the side of the reel. The left hand grasps the butt of the rod solidly, almost at the end.

As the lure hits the water, drop the butt of the rod in the whip socket; hold the rod as shown for retrieving the line or playing the fish.

one hundred yards of 30-pound backing. Big streamer flies will attract a striper on a running tide at dusk. Hook a big one and you may still be there at the break of day. The season is from May to October.

Trolling requires a rod of 6- to 12-ounce tip and a free-spool reel with two hundred yards of 6-, 9-, or 12-thread linen or nylon line. Troll a spinner baited with worms or an eel-skin rig, or a bass plug, and troll slowly.

If you like surf casting from the beach, then you need surf-rod tips six or seven feet long with a thirty-inch butt, a free-spool reel, and two hundred yards of 9- or 12-thread line. For lures, there is a nice variety from metal squids to feather jigs and plugs.

When the stripers are running along the eastern shores, the Pacific salmon are coming in to spawn in the Northwest. The hysteria is about even. The largest salmon is the chinook, called king salmon in Washington and Alaska, and referred to as Tyee salmon in British Columbia. Up the Columbia and other great rivers of the Northwest comes this monster; in August and September, the fishermen go in for great salmon derbies. The biggest chinook ever caught on hook and line weighed more than 97 pounds.

These great fish are caught while trolling, spinning, and mooching. What is a "moocher"? A moocher is a saltwater troller in Puget Sound. A moocher differs from a troller in that he puts out many yards of line, using little weight, and depends on the length of the line and the slowness of the boat to put the bait on the bottom. He rows the boat with short strokes that make the bait dart on and near the bottom. This strategy often catches the large salmon.

In fact, wherever you go in this broad land, there is plenty of fishing pretty close at hand. No angler needs to go beyond his own state borders to meet at least a few game fish, and deep-sea fishing awaits him along the nearest coastline.

Chapter 14

FISHING THROUGH THE ICE

By keeping in mind a few simple tricks, you can bring home as many panfish during the winter months as the best catches you've had throughout the summer. One of the first things to remember about ice fishing, however, is to dress for it. To keep your feet warm on the ice, fit two or three inner soles, cut from an old felt hat, into each boot. Wear two pairs of light-weight woolen socks, as these are warmer than a single heavy pair, and take along several pairs of woolen gloves or mittens, so you will always have a dry pair. Waterproofed leather choppers' mitts worn over the woolen gloves afford added protection when handling cold, wet lines and fish.

ADVICE FROM AN ANGLER: During moderately cold weather, holes chopped in the ice for fishing may be kept from freezing over at night by placing snow-filled pails in them. As a further precaution against freezing, one fisherman inserts a lath in each pail and ties a cloth to it. The cloth serves as a marker, and the slightest breeze causes the pail to rock, preventing ice formation.

An efficient and inexpensive tool for chopping holes through the ice is made by welding a wide chisel blade to a length of pipe. (You can also purchase an ice auger.) A hole is drilled at the top end of the pipe for attaching a leather thong or a strong cord, and a loop tied in the end of the thong is slipped over the wrist, so that the tool will not fall

through the hole if it is dropped. Make the holes in the ice about fifteen inches in diameter. And flare out the edges on the underside, so that the sharp ice will not fray the line. After cutting the hole, use an old tea strainer to skim the pieces of ice from the water, as shown.

In winter, the location of the fish and whether or not they are biting cannot be judged by the usual rules, such as wind, barometric pressure, or water temperature. The fish seem to show the most action between 10:00 A.M. and 4:00 P.M., but this is not a hard-and-fast rule. If the water is shallow, the fish will take to the deepest holes they can find. Other good fishing spots are near weeds in six to twenty feet of water, off rocky points, in sheltered

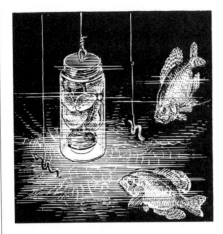

In some lakes and rivers, fishing through the ice is best after dark. To attract the fish to the bait, lower a tightly capped fruit jar containing a small lighted flashlight into the water, and fish around the light. Use stones to weight the jar so it will sink, and tie a line around the rim of the jar or tie it to a screw eye soldered to the jar cover. Another way to attract fish at night or in deep water during the daytime is to tie a small perfume vial to each line just above the baited hook. The inside of the vial is coated with luminous paint, and the vial is capped tightly. The glow of the paint will bring curious fish to the vicinity of the bait. To attract fish to your bait in the daytime, drop a handful of crushed oyster shells through a hole in the ice. The shells will glitter on the lake bottom and lure the fish to the location of your bait. These shells usually are available at poultry-supply dealers.

coves, over sandbars, and around spring holes in the lake bottom. An excellent location for catching pike and walleyes is frequently found off the mouth of a stream that flows into the main body of water.

Panfish bite daintily during the winter, usually nibbling only at the head or tail of a worm. To outsmart the nibblers, fasten a panfish hook to each end of an eight-inch nylon leader and knot the center of the leader to form a loop for tying to the line. Then simply impale the ends of the worm on the hooks.

Although worms and minnows are the most widely used baits, they are not necessarily the best for panfishing through ice.

ADVICE FROM AN ANGLER: To retard the freezing over of holes cut in the ice for fishing, pour enough glycerin or olive oil on the water to form a thin film. This will keep the holes open for some time.

Here are some bait suggestions for surefire results. When fish won't take any other bait, use winter-killed honeybees, which can be obtained from a local beekeeper. Of course, if you can find a wasps' nest in the woods, the cold, dormant wasps will work as well as bees. Another bait that will give satisfactory results is the mealworm, which can be had from just about any feed store or grain elevator. Leeches are an excellent bait for game fish and panfish, and they may be purchased from drug-supply houses. For one of the best winter baits, use small bullheads, with the

Although bait minnows can be trapped as easily in winter as in summer, most wire and plastic traps freeze under the ice. A serviceable trap can be made from a large fruit jar and the upper half of a quart milk bottle, as shown. Set the trap in shallow channels where the current is swift, anchoring it between two large stones so it is not washed away. The mouth of the trap should face downstream. Several of these traps, baited with raw oatmeal or bread crumbs, will keep you well supplied with minnows all winter long. the slot should be smoothed with fine abrasive paper to avoid marring the finish on the rod tip.

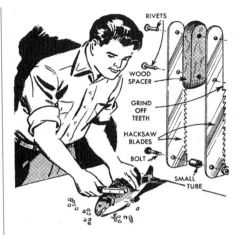

Discarded power-hacksaw blades can be used by fishermen to make a fish scaler. Two pieces of blade 7½ inches long are required, and the teeth are ground off for a distance of 4 inches to form a handle. Note, however, that the teeth point in the opposite directions, so that the maximum scraping effect is obtained. A wood spacer, which is sawed and sanded to fit the contour of a handle, is riveted between the blades. To complete the scaler, a tube of a length equal to the width of the wooden spacer is inserted where indicated.

sharp spines and fins snipped off. Game fish are attracted by the blood and, quickly noticing the lack of sharp spines, attack at once. As a bait for large pike and walleyes, there is little better than a four- or five-inch sucker, chub, or perch, and one or two small, red glass beads slipped onto a No. 12 or 14 gold-plated hook will often take panfish in the winter.

CALL FOR CONSERVATION

By Ted Williams, (1918-2002), a legendary baseball player with the Boston Red Sox and an avid sport fisherman, named to the International Game Fish Association Hall of Fame in 2000

I have been asked a hundred times if I can compare the highlights of my career in baseball to the thrills of fishing. It's a tough question to answer because I've devoted myself to both sports and they're fundamentally different.

Is making a good cast to a fish and fighting it skillfully similar to hitting a home run? I'd be lying if I said yes. There's no feeling in the world comparable to hitting a baseball out of the park in front of a home-town crowd in a big game.

Yet, I firmly believe there's no greater outdoor activity available to human beings than sportfishing. You're never too young or too old to participate, and the excitement, pleasure and challenge are always there. It doesn't matter if the fish you're after is a 2-ounce bluegill or a 200-pound marlin. If the tackle is right for the size of fish, it's always a sporting proposition, and a damn fine one at that.

Like many lucky Americans, I've had the good fortune to fish for walleye and muskie in the Midwest, bonefish and tarpon in Florida's saltwater flats, marlin and tuna in the ocean, salmon and trout in streams from Maine to the Flathead River system in Montana, and bluegill and bass in the Arkansas River, near Little Rock, and throughout the South. I guess you could call me a Will Rogers fisherman; I've never met a fish I didn't like.

With 50 years of angling under my belt, and many more ahead, I know I'm not likely to grow tired of the sport. The reason? Whenever I see a young boy fishing with his dad I can't help but notice the magic in his face as he feels a fish pulling on the end of his line. I think I still have some of this kid-at-heart attitude about fishing with me, as I think most fishermen do, regardless of how gray they might be getting around the edges.

Like most fishermen my age, I started fishing with a bamboo pole as a California kid, and progressed from there. I didn't take it up seriously until much later in life. It was tough to break away for a day or so of fishing when I was playing baseball, although I did my best. Occasionally, I was able to sample the fishing in cities I played ball in, but this was rare. Mostly, I had to wait for the off-season.

When I began fishing, more than half a century ago, the tackle wasn't nearly as sophisticated as it is today. In fact, it was pretty crude. Modern reels, for example, are stronger, more reliable, and equipped with smoother drags than anything available when I started.

Rods have equally improved. My first rod, as mentioned, was made of split bamboo. This material was replaced by fiberglass, which gave way to graphite, boron, and synthetic composites. New rods are lighter, more powerful, and much less tiring to use. Monofilament fishing line, of course, is a genuine marvel of science compared to the old silkworm gut leader and braided linen line I started out with.

Despite all the technological advances I've witnessed, I've never lost sight of the fact that hard-fighting fish, even big offshore monsters, could always be whipped by using the right tackle. And that tackle didn't have to be heavy duty, either. Keep the pressure on, with just the right touch and skill, and the biggest tarpon or marlin in the world will eventually tire out and give up the fight.

I guess I could say the gods of fishing, whoever they may be, have smiled on me, because I've caught more than a thousand Atlantic salmon. (I've caught about 1000 tarpon and bonefish, too.) I don't keep the big Atlantics anymore, although I did in years past when they were more plentiful. Despite the large numbers of the fish I've caught, the next one will be just as exciting as the first one, because each is a great adventure in its own way.

It's a funny thing about releasing a fish. The first time you set a big one free feels kind of strange, maybe even a little painful. But the next one is easier and after that, they're all easy. You don't have to have a dead fish to prove you caught it. You know you did, and that's all that's important.

I release all my bonefish, tarpon, and all but a fraction of my Atlantic salmon. Why? Because it's clear to me, and to anyone who's been fishing for the last few decades, that size and quantity of gamefish are far below the levels they used to be. Do the fish survive after being caught? Experts disagree on the subject. Obviously, if you manhandle the fish in the process of pulling the hook out, the chances go down. Lately, I've taken to filing the barbs off of my hooks, which makes it easy to release a prized fish. I caught and released the largest Atlantic salmon of my life, a 30-pound-plus female, on a barbless hook.

When I began angling seriously more than 30 years ago, the fishing was pretty good and I made up my mind to learn everything I could about this fantastic sport. As the years went by, I discovered that not everything I learned was good news.

Oldtimers told me that Atlantic salmon fishing was twice as good when they were younger. I shrugged at this, because I thought it was still pretty good in the mid-1950s. But it wasn't too long before I began to notice a change. Fewer fish appeared each year and they were noticeably smaller. I began to make a journal of my catches to chart the gradual change, but I gave it up before too long. Within a few years, the run of salmon was down to a trickle. You didn't need a written record to note the change; it was like night and day.

Generation after generation of Atlantic salmon were netted wholesale by commercial fisherman looking for an easy catch. They simply set nets up at the mouths of rivers and caught every fish headed towards its instinctive spawning grounds. Many of Maine's most productive salmon streams—and those in the Canadian Provinces, too—were wiped out completely. I don't mean that the fish were so depleted that sportfishermen were less likely to catch them. I mean that no fish made it to the spawning ground for several consecutive years, no eggs were laid, no salmonoids hatched and no salmon headed out to the ocean to reach adulthood and someday return. None. Zero.

Bonefish and tarpon suffered during this time as well, and are still suffering. The difference with this fish is that they aren't the primary target of the commercial fishermen. They are an accidental catch. Commercial fishermen are becoming too efficient, using miles of netting and stripping the water of fish wherever they roam. They aren't actively seeking to kill bonefish, kingfish, marlin, swordfish, sailfish, and several others, but the result is the same.

Gamefish or sportfish aren't the only species to suffer in recent years. Most fishermen are all too aware of species depletion in natural stocks of striped bass, snook, redfish, grouper, several kinds of tuna, sea bass, salmon, steelhead trout on the West Coast and many others. Sportsmen's groups and conservation agencies are working together on this to raise public awareness of the problem, to restore threatened stocks, and to get legislation passed to ensure the continuation of current species for future generations. Some of the work done in this area is controversial. Commercial fishermen feel pressured. Even some sportfishermen feel that government regulation goes against the grain of a sport that is among the purest expressions of freedom.

I believe it's time that we made saltwater licenses mandatory for all anglers, both commercial and sport. I know that some states already have a saltwater license, but what good does it do if one state is regulated and the neighboring one isn't?

Fishermen with a mind to circumvent the license law just pull into a dock in an unlicensed state and unload the ill-gotten catch. This type of thing happens every day. Without a federal license and certain nationwide regulations, depletion will continue and hoped for improvement will be impossible.

I'm basically conservative by nature and against government meddling whenever possible. But I've seen drastic changes in fish population in my lifetime and they haven't been for the better. The problem with licenses, of course, is enforcement. What good are they if no one checks? This is where the fee comes in. It should be written into the legislation tat money collected for saltwater licenses goes for hard-nosed law enforcement and restoration work.

My second point concerns sportfish in general. I think a study should be done to determine exactly what a sportfish is and ban their commercial sale. This opens the proverbial can of worms, because not everyone agrees with what a sportfish is. My list would include all the marlin, swordfish, striped bass, bonefish, tarpon, permit, redfish, sailfish and, to be honest, other species in danger of depletion. In addition, I believe bluefin tuna and Atlantic salmon should be closely watched and, perhaps, commercial fishing near shore temporarily suspended.

My final point concerns pollution. Sure, we've got to do something with our garbage and industrial waste, but pouring it into the nearest body of water isn't the solution. Unrestricted dumping in rivers, lakes, and coastal waters harms the habitat and harms the fish. You don't have to be a fisherman to understand this; it's plain to anyone.

Once again, I don't have an easy answer in mind and studies by experts and politicians needs to be done. But once those studies are completed, I'd get behind them to make sure we take the steps necessary to create enough clean water to ensure fishing for future generations. Corrective measures this late in the game may prove to be harsh medicine to some special interest groups, but there's no easy solution and not everyone's going to be happy. Is this too strong a stand? I don't think so. In fact, I believe, more and more fisherman should move to the forefront of the fight against pollution and the cleaning up of the waterways in this country.

Despite the cloud that seems to be hanging over some areas of the fishing scene, there are a number of bright spots, too. I have good feelings about the future of the sport, because I think we're finally beginning to turn the corner. In freshwater fishing, trout and bass stocks are actually better in many regions than they were 20 years ago. The Great Lakes have made an amazing comeback and serve as a wonderful example of what can be done when people get serious.

Lake trout, brown trout, and Pacific salmon are providing better fishing today than many thought possible a few years ago. Even the Atlantic salmon is on the comeback trail in Maine and a couple of other New England states. Also, striped bass and walleye have recently become increasingly important sport species in freshwater lakes throughout the country.

State conservation agencies and private groups, such as Trout Unlimited, Atlantic Salmon Federation, Federation of Fly Fishers, International Gamefish Association, and the Isaak Walton League, are more active and even winning a few battles. I support their efforts in trying to bring intelligent management to the world of fishing, and I think every fisherman should, too.

I've done as much fishing as I could do in this great country of ours and I've enjoyed every minute of it. Fishing has given me a lot in life and the reason I've made such strong statements regarding its future is that I'd like to give something back. We've got the best country in the world for fishing right here in America. Let's do everything we can to keep it that way.

—MAY, 1989

INDEX